FASTING: A BAHÁ'Í HANDBOOK

. . . as the sun and moon constitute the brightest and most prominent luminaries in the heavens, similarly in the heaven of the religion of God two shining orbs have been ordained – fasting and prayer . . . fasting is its sun, prayer, its moon.

BAHÁ'U'LLÁH

Fasting

The Sun and its Moons

A BAHÁ'Í HANDBOOK

compiled by

DUANE L. HERRMANN

GEORGE RONALD
OXFORD

GEORGE RONALD, Publisher
46 High Street, Kidlington, Oxford, OX5 2DN
This compilation © Duane L. Herrmann
All Rights Reserved

British Library Cataloguing in Publication Data

Fasting
  1. Bahai life. Fasting
  I. Title
  297′.89446

  ISBN 0–85398–280–5
  ISBN 0–85398–281–3 Pbk

Grateful acknowledgement is made for permission to quote from the following works: T. Armistead, 'An Open Letter to new Bahá'ís regarding the Fast', *The American Bahá'í*, February 1986, © National Spiritual Assembly of the Bahá'ís of the United States; *Bahá'í News*, January and April 1950, © National Spiritual Assembly of the Bahá'ís of the United States; Mírzá Abu'l-Faḍl Gulpáygání, *Miracles and Metaphors*, Kalimát Press, © 1981 Juan Ricardo Cole; Ruḥiyyih Rabbání, *Desire of the World*, George Ronald, © 1982 Ruḥiyyih Rabbání; Adib Taherzadeh, *The Revelation of Bahá'u'lláh, 'Akká, The Early Years*, George Ronald, © 1983 Adib Taherzadeh.

Set by Photoprint in Bembo 12 on 13 point
Printed and bound in Great Britain by
Billing & Sons Ltd., Worcester

Contents

FROM THE WRITINGS OF
BAHÁ'U'LLÁH

THINK not that We have revealed unto you a mere code of laws. Nay, rather, We have unsealed the choice Wine with the fingers of might and power. To this beareth witness that which the Pen of Revelation hath revealed. Meditate upon this, O men of insight![1]

WE have commanded you to pray and fast from the beginning of maturity; this is ordained by God, your Lord and the Lord of your forefathers. He has exempted from this those who are weak from illness or age, as a bounty from His Presence, and He is the Forgiving, the Generous.[2]

WE have enjoined upon you fasting during a brief period, and at its close have designated for you Naw-Rúz as a feast . . . The traveller, the ailing, those who are with child or giving suck, are not bound by the fast . . . Abstain from food and drink, from sunrise to sundown, and beware lest desire deprive you of this grace that is appointed in the Book.[3]

CONSIDER thou and call to mind the time when

Muḥammad appeared. He said, and His word is the truth: 'Pilgrimage to the House* is a service due to God.'† And likewise are the daily prayer, fasting, and the laws which shone forth above the horizon of the Book of God, the Lord of the World and the true Educator of the peoples and kindreds of the earth. It is incumbent upon everyone to obey Him in whatsoever God hath ordained; and whosoever denieth Him hath disbelieved in God, in His verses, in His Messengers and in His Books.4

IN another sense, by the terms 'sun', 'moon', and 'stars' are meant such laws and teachings as have been established and proclaimed in every Dispensation, such as the laws of prayer and fasting. These have, according to the law of the Qur'án, been regarded, when the beauty of the Prophet Muḥammad had passed beyond the veil, as the most fundamental and binding laws of His dispensation. To this testify the texts of the traditions and chronicles, which, on account of their being widely known, need not be referred to here. Nay rather, in every Dispensation the law concerning prayer hath been emphasized and universally enforced. To this testify the recorded traditions ascribed to the lights that have emanated from the Day-star of Truth, the essence of the Prophet Muḥammad.

The traditions established the fact that in all Dispensations the law of prayer hath constituted a fundamental element of the Revelation of all the Prophets of God – a law the form and the manner of which hath been

* Mecca.
† Qur'án 3:91.

adapted to the varying requirements of every age. Inasmuch as every subsequent Revelation hath abolished the manners, habits, and teachings that have been clearly, specifically, and firmly established by the former Dispensation, these have accordingly been symbolically expressed in terms of 'sun' and 'moon'. 'That He might prove you, which of you excel in deeds.'*

Moreover, in the traditions the terms 'sun' and 'moon' have been applied to prayer and fasting, even as it is said: 'Fasting is illumination, prayer is light.' One day, a well-known divine came to visit Us. While We were conversing with him, he referred to the above-quoted tradition. He said: 'Inasmuch as fasting causeth the heat of the body to increase, it hath therefore been likened unto the light of the sun; and as the prayer of the night-season refresheth man, it hath been compared unto the radiance of the moon.' Thereupon We realized that that poor man had not been favoured with a single drop of the ocean of true understanding, and had strayed far from the burning Bush of divine wisdom. We then politely observed to him saying: 'The interpretation your honour hath given to this tradition is the one current amongst the people. Could it not be interpreted differently?' He asked Us: 'What could it be?' We made reply: 'Muḥammad, the Seal of the Prophets, and the most distinguished of God's chosen Ones, hath likened the Dispensation of the Qur'án unto heaven, by reason of its loftiness, its paramount influence, its majesty, and the fact that it comprehendeth all religions. And as the sun and moon constitute the brightest and most prominent luminaries in the heavens, similarly in the heaven of the religion of God two shining orbs have been ordained – fasting and prayer.'⁵

* Qur'án 67:2.

O SHAYKH, O thou who hast surrendered thy will to God! By self-surrender and perpetual union with God is meant that men should merge their will wholly in the Will of God, and regard their desires as utter nothingness beside His Purpose. Whatsoever the Creator commandeth His creatures to observe, the same must they diligently, and with the utmost joy and eagerness, arise and fulfil. They should in no wise allow their fancy to obscure their judgment, neither should they regard their own imaginings as the voice of the Eternal. In the Prayer of Fasting We have revealed: 'Should Thy Will decree that out of Thy mouth these words proceed and be addressed unto them, "Observe, for My Beauty's sake, the fast, O people, and set no limit to its duration," I swear by the majesty of Thy glory, that every one of them will faithfully observe it, will abstain from whatsoever will violate Thy law, and will continue to do so until they yield up their souls unto Thee.' In this consisteth the complete surrender of one's will to the Will of God. Meditate on this, that thou mayest drink in the waters of everlasting life which flow through the words of the Lord of all mankind, and mayest testify that the one true God hath ever been immeasurably exalted above His creatures. He, verily, is the Incomparable, the Ever-Abiding, the Omniscient, the All-Wise. The station of absolute self-surrender transcendeth, and will ever remain exalted above, every other station.

It behoveth thee to consecrate thyself to the Will of God. Whatsoever hath been revealed in His Tablets is but a reflection of His Will. So complete must be thy consecration, that every trace of worldly desire will be washed from thine heart. This is the meaning of true unity.

Do thou beseech God to enable thee to remain

steadfast in this path, and to aid thee to guide the peoples of the world to Him Who is the manifest and sovereign Ruler, Who hath revealed Himself in a distinct attire, Who giveth utterance to a Divine and specific Message. This is the essence of faith and certitude.[6]

FROM THE WRITINGS OF
'ABDU'L-BAHÁ

O ARMY of God! A letter signed jointly by all of you hath been received. It was most eloquent and full of flavour, and reading it was a delight.

Ye had written of the fasting month. Fortunate are ye to have obeyed the commandment of God, and kept this fast during the holy season. For this material fast is an outer token of the spiritual fast; it is a symbol of self-restraint, the withholding of oneself from all appetites of the self, taking on the characteristics of the spirit, being carried away by the breathings of heaven and catching fire from the love of God.[1]

O THOU spiritual friend! Thou hast asked the wisdom of prayer. Know thou that prayer is indispensable and obligatory, and man under no pretext whatsoever is excused from performing the prayer unless he be mentally unsound, or an insurmountable obstacle prevent him. The wisdom of prayer is this: That it causeth a connection between the servant and the True One, because in that state man with all heart and soul turneth his face towards His Highness the Almighty, seeking His association and desiring His love and compassion. The greatest happiness for a lover is to converse with his beloved, and the greatest gift for a seeker is to become familiar with the object of his longing; that is why with every soul who is attracted to the Kingdom of God, his greatest hope is to find an opportunity to entreat and supplicate before his Beloved, appeal for His mercy and grace and be immersed in the ocean of His utterance, goodness and generosity.

Besides all this, prayer and fasting is the cause of awakening and mindfulness and conducive to protection and preservation from tests . . .[2]

THE nineteen-day fast is a duty to be observed by all. All should abstain from eating and drinking from sunrise to sunset. This fast is conducive to the spiritual development of the individual. The Greatest Name should be read every day.[3]

FROM TABLE TALKS BY 'ABDU'L-BAHÁ

QUESTION: *What Divine wisdom is there in fasting?*

The Divine wisdom in fasting is manifold. Among them is this: As during those days [i.e. the period of fasting which the followers afterward observe] the Manifestation of the Sun of Reality, through Divine inspiration, is engaged in the descent [revealing] of Verses, the instituting of Divine Law and the arrangement of teachings, through excessive occupation and intense attraction there remains no condition or time for eating and drinking. For example, when his holiness Moses went to Mount Tur (Sinai) and there engaged in instituting the Law of God, he fasted forty days. For the purpose of awakening and admonishing the people of Israel, fasting was enjoined upon them.

Likewise, his holiness Christ, in the beginning of instituting the Spiritual Law, the systematizing of the teachings and the arrangement of counsels, for forty days abstained from eating and drinking. In the beginning the disciples and Christians fasted. Later the assemblages of the chief Christians changed fasting into lenten observances.

Likewise the Qur'án having descended in the month Ramaḍan, fasting during that month became a duty.

In like manner his holiness the Supreme [the Báb], in the beginning of the Manifestation, through the excessive effect of descending Verses, passed days in which his nourishment was reduced to tea only.

Likewise, the Blessed Beauty [Bahá'u'lláh], when busy with instituting the Divine Teachings and during

the days when the Verses [the Word of God] descended
continuously, through the great effect of the Verses and
the throbbing of the heart, took no food except the least
amount.

The purpose is this: In order to follow the Divine
Manifestations and for the purpose of admonition and
the commemoration of their state, it became incumbent
upon the people to fast during those days. For every
sincere soul who has a beloved longs to experience that
state in which his beloved is. If his beloved is in a state of
sorrow, he desires sorrow; if in a state of joy, he desires
joy; if in a state of rest, he desires rest; if in a state of
trouble, he desires trouble.

Now, since in this Millennial Day, his holiness the
Supreme fasted many days, and the Blessed Beauty took
but little food or drink, it becomes necessary that the
friends should follow that example. For thus saith He in
the *Tablet of Visitation*: They, the believers, 'who, for
love of Thee, have observed all whereunto they were
bidden'.

This is one wisdom of the wisdoms of fasting.

The second wisdom is this: Fasting is the cause of
awakening man. The heart becomes tender and the
spirituality of man increases. This is produced by the
fact that man's thoughts will be confined to the
commemoration of God, and through this awakening
and stimulation surely ideal advancements follow.

Third wisdom: Fasting is of two kinds, material and
spiritual. The material fasting is abstaining from food or
drink, that is, from the appetites of the body. But
spiritual, ideal fasting is this, that man abstain from
selfish passions, from negligence and from satanic
animal traits. Therefore, material fasting is a token of
the spiritual fasting. That is:

O Divine Providence! As I am abstaining from bodily desires

and not occupied with eating and drinking, even so purify and sanctify my heart from the love of anyone save Thyself and shield and protect my soul from corrupt desires and satanic qualities so that my spirit may commune with the breaths of holiness and fast from the mention of all else besides Thee.[1]

FASTING is a symbol. Fasting signifies abstinence from lust. Physical fasting is a symbol of that abstinence, and is a reminder; that is, just as a person abstains from physical appetites, he is to abstain from self-appetites and self-desires. But mere abstention from food has no effect on the spirit. It is only a symbol, a reminder. Otherwise it is of no importance. Fasting for this purpose does not mean entire abstinence from food. The golden rule as to food is, do not take too much or too little. Moderation is necessary. There is a sect in India who practise extreme abstinence, and gradually reduce their food until they exist on almost nothing. But their intelligence suffers. A man is not fit to do service for God with brain or body if he is weakened by lack of food. He cannot see clearly.[2]

FROM LETTERS WRITTEN
ON BEHALF OF
SHOGHI EFFENDI

THOSE unwarranted practices, in connection with the sacrament of baptism, of communion, of confession of sins, of asceticism, of priestly dominion, of elaborate ceremonies, of holy war and of polygamy, have one and all been rigidly suppressed by the Pen of Bahá'u'lláh; whilst the rigidity and rigour of certain observances, such as fasting, which are necessary to the devotional life of the individual, have been considerably abated. [1]

THERE are also no obligatory prayers for the Fast. But there are some specific ones revealed by Bahá'u'lláh for that purpose. [2]

CERTAIN laws, such as fasting, obligatory prayers, the consent of the parents before marriage, avoidance of alcoholic drinks, monogamy, should be regarded by all believers as universally and vitally applicable at the present time. [3]

As regards fasting, it constitutes, together with the obligatory prayers, the two pillars that sustain the revealed Law of God. They act as stimulants to the soul, strengthen, revive and purify it, and thus insure its steady development.

The ordinance of fasting is, as is the case with these three prayers (the daily obligatory ones), a spiritual and vital obligation enjoined by Bahá'u'lláh upon every believer who has attained the age of fifteen. In the Aqdas He thus writes: 'We have commanded you to pray and fast from the beginning of maturity; this is ordained by God, your Lord and the Lord of your forefathers. He has exempted from this those who are weak from illness or age, as a bounty from His Presence, and He is the Forgiving, the Generous.' And in another passage He says: 'We have enjoined upon you fasting during a brief period, and at its close have designated for you Naw-Rúz as a feast . . . The traveller, the ailing, those who are with child or giving suck, are not bound by the fast . . . Abstain from food and drink, from sunrise to sundown, and beware lest desire deprive you of this grace that is appointed in the Book.'

Also in the 'Questions and Answers' that form an appendix to the Aqdas, Bahá'u'lláh reveals the following: 'Verily, I say that God has appointed a great station for fasting and prayer. But during good health its benefit is evident, and when one is ill, it is not permissible to fulfil them.' Concerning the age of maturity, He reveals in the appendix of that same book: 'The age of maturity is in the fifteenth year: women and men are alike in this respect.'

Regarding the vital character and importance of the Divine ordinances and laws, and the necessity of complete obedience to them by the believers, we thus read in the *Gleanings*, p. 175: 'Know verily that the essence of justice and the source thereof are both embodied in the ordinances prescribed by Him Who is

the Manifestation of the Self of God amongst men, if ye
be of them that recognize this truth. He doth verily
incarnate the highest, the infallible standard of justice
unto all creation. Were his law to be such as to strike
terror into the hearts of all that are in heaven and on
earth, that law is naught but manifest justice. The fears
and agitation which the revelation of this law provoke
in men's hearts should indeed be likened to the cries of
the suckling babe weaned from his mother's milk, if ye
be of them that perceive . . .'

The fasting period, which lasts nineteen days starting
as a rule from the second of March every year and
ending on the twentieth of the same month, involves
complete abstention from food and drink from sunrise
till sunset. It is essentially a period of meditation and
prayer, of spiritual recuperation, during which the
believer must strive to make the necessary readjust-
ments in his inner life, and to refresh and reinvigorate
the spiritual forces latent in his soul. Its significance and
purpose are, therefore, fundamentally spiritual in character. Fasting is symbolic, and a reminder of abstinence
from selfish and carnal desires.4

REGARDING the nineteen-day fast; its observance has been
enjoined by Bahá'u'lláh upon all the believers, once they
attain the age of fifteen and until they reach seventy.
Children of all countries, nationalities and classes, who
are fifteen years old are under this obligation. It matters
not whether they mature later in one country than in
another. The command of Bahá'u'lláh is universal,
irrespective of any variance in the age of maturity in
different countries and among different peoples.

In the 'Aqdas' Bahá'u'lláh permits certain exceptions to this general obligation of fasting, among them are included those who do hard work, such as workers in heavy industries.

But while a universal obligation, the observance of the nineteen-day fast has been made by Bahá'u'lláh the sole responsibility of the individual believer. No Assembly has the right to enforce it on the friends, or to hold anybody responsible for not observing it. The believer is free, however, to ask the advice of his Assembly as to the circumstances that would justify him to conscientiously break such a fast. But he is by no means required to do so.[5]

WITH reference to your son's request for advice regarding the observance of the Bahá'í Fast; much as the Guardian realizes the difficulty which a believer of his position, attending a military school, will have to encounter if he wishes to *strictly conform* to the regulations of the Fast, he nevertheless would advise him to make every effort to obtain from the school authorities the necessary permission. In case his request is refused the only alternative for him would be to obey his superior.[6]

IF, however, you find your health affected by keeping the Fast the Guardian would advise you to consult a physician, and if he tells you you are unable to fast then of course, you should abstain from doing so.[7]

REGARDING your question concerning the Fast: Travellers are exempt from fasting, but if they want to fast while they are travelling, they are free to do so. You are exempt the whole period of your travel, not just the hours you are in a train or car, etc. If one eats unconsciously during the fasting hours, this is not breaking the Fast as it is an accident. The age limit is seventy years, but if one desires to fast after the age limit is passed, and is strong enough to, one is free to do so. If during the Fast period a person falls ill and is unable to fast, but recovers before the fast period is over, he can start to fast again and continue until the end. Of course the Fast, as you know, can only be kept during the month set aside for that purpose. 8

KEEPING the Fast is enjoined upon all Bahá'ís, regardless of nationality; it has a very salutary effect both physically and spiritually, and the friends should realize Bahá'u'lláh never would have instituted it if it were detrimental to the health. The Master referred to the Fast in talks to pilgrims, and some Tablets, but most material on this subject is not yet translated.9

HE is indeed pleased to know that the book of *Prayers and Meditations* by Bahá'u'lláh has been out in time to enable the friends to read it during the Fast, and he has every hope that the perusal of such a precious volume will help to deepen, *more than any other publication*, the spirit of devotion and faith in the friends, and thus charge them with all the spiritual power they require for the accomplishment of their tremendous duties towards the Cause . . .[10]

It is difficult for us to do things because they are so very different from what we are used to, not because the thing itself is particularly difficult. With you, and indeed most Bahá'ís, who are now, as adults, accepting this glorious Faith, no doubt some of the ordinances, like fasting and daily prayer, are hard to understand and obey at first. But we must always think that these things are given to all men for a thousand years to come. For Bahá'í children who see these things practised in the home, they will be as natural and necessary a thing as going to church on Sunday was to the more pious generation of Christians.

Bahá'u'lláh would not have given us these things if they would not greatly benefit us, and, like children who are sensible enough to realize their father is wise and does what is good for them, we must obey these ordinances even though at first we may not see any need for them. As we obey them we will gradually come to see in ourselves the benefits they confer.[11]

He feels that if you consider it too much of a strain to keep the Fast you should not do so. Bahá'u'lláh has exempted people who are travellers at the time; if you could keep it the days you are not travelling, and thus partake of its bounty, it would be advisable, but it is not essential.[12]

MARCH 21, as the Master once explained, is the time of year when the climate is most moderate the world over. It is suited, therefore, to the New Year, which in our Faith comes after the month of fasting. The Fast itself Bahá'u'lláh made easy by choosing the time when the days and nights everywhere are most equal.[13]

. . . OF course the Fast must either be kept entirely or not at all. If a physician advises, for reasons of health, against keeping it, then the person can give it up.[14]

DIRECTIVES FROM
THE UNIVERSAL HOUSE OF
JUSTICE

From *A Synopsis and Codification of the Kitáb-i-Aqdas*
SECTION IV.B.

(1) The sublime station occupied by fasting in the Bahá'í Revelation.

(2) The period of fasting commences with the termination of the Intercalary Days, and ends with the Naw-Rúz Festival.

(3) Abstinence from food and drink,* from sunrise to sunset, is obligatory.

(4) Fasting is binding on men and women on attaining the age of maturity, which is fixed at 15.

(5) Exemption from fasting is granted to:
    (a) Travellers
        i. Provided the journey exceeds 9 hours.
        ii. Those travelling on foot, provided the journey exceeds 2 hours.
        iii. Those who break their journey for less than 19 days.

---

* Note 16 to the Synopsis states:

> In one of His Tablets 'Abdu'l-Bahá, after stating that fasting consists of abstinence from food and drink, categorically says that smoking is a form of 'drink'. (In Arabic the verb 'drink' applies equally to smoking.)

In a letter referring to this passage the Universal House of Justice states:

> The prohibition of smoking as an aspect of fasting, as explained in Note 16, on page 59 of the *Synopsis and Codification of the Kitáb-i-Aqdas* has not yet been applied in the West and therefore the friends should not make an issue of it. (*From a letter dated 24 February 1978 to a National Spiritual Assembly*)

iv. Those who break their journey during the Fast at a place where they are to stay 19 days are exempt from fasting only for the first three days from their arrival.

v. Those who reach home during the Fast must commence fasting from the day of their arrival.*

(b) Those who are ill.

(c) Those who are over 70.

(d) Women who are with child.

(e) Women who are nursing.

(f) Women in their courses, provided they perform their ablutions and repeat a specifically revealed verse 95 times a day.*†

(g) Those who are engaged in heavy labour, who are advised to show respect for the law by using discretion and restraint when availing themselves of the exemption.

---

* 'It has become apparent from a number of questions we have received that many believers are not clear which are those laws already binding upon the Bahá'ís in the West. We therefore feel it is timely to clarify the situation and the simplest way is to state those laws listed in the *Synopsis and Codification of the Kitáb-i-Aqdas* which are *not* at present binding upon the friends in the western world. For ease of reference we give the numbers of the sections listed . . .

IV.B.(5)(a) The definition of travellers for the purpose of exemption from fasting. Instead of these definitions the believers in the West should observe the following guidance given by the beloved Guardian's secretary on his behalf:
    'Travellers are exempt from fasting, but if they want to fast while they are travelling, they are free to do so. You are exempt the whole period of your travel, not just the hours you are in a train or car, etc . . .'

IV.B.(5)(f) The law regarding the exemption from fasting granted to women in their courses.'

(*From a letter dated 9 June 1974 written by the Universal House of Justice to a National Spiritual Assembly*)

† Note 5 to the *Synopsis* states:

The specifically revealed verse, which is to be repeated 95 times a day between one noon and the next, is '*Glorified be God, the Lord of Splendour and Beauty.*'

(6) Vowing to fast (in a month other than the one prescribed for fasting) is permissible. Vows which profit mankind are however preferable in the sight of God.

From Letters Written on Behalf of
The Universal House of Justice

As Bahá'u'lláh has stated in the Kitáb-i-Aqdas: 'We have commanded you to pray and fast from the beginning of maturity; this is ordained by God, your Lord and the Lord of your forefathers . . .' '. . . We have enjoined upon you fasting during a brief period, and at its close have designated for you Naw-Rúz as a feast . . . Abstain from food and drink, from sunrise to sundown, and beware lest desire deprive you of this grace that is appointed in the Book.' The Fast is thus seen to be a fundamental element in the spiritual life and growth of each Bahá'í, sharing this distinction with the daily obligatory prayers.[1]

In the *Synopsis and Codification of the Laws and Ordinances of the Kitáb-i-Aqdas*, p. 39, you will note there are exemptions for 'Those who are ill', and 'Those who are engaged in heavy labour, . . .' As you are aware, keeping the Fast is a spiritual obligation left to the conscience of the individual believer.

Also in a letter written on behalf of the beloved Guardian to an individual believer it is said:

. . . of course the Fast must either be kept entirely or not at all. If a physician advises, for reasons of health, against keeping it, then the person can give it up.

Thus if a physician advises that fasting in extreme heat will produce a condition detrimental to one's health, one would be excused from keeping the Fast.[2]

CONCERNING the fasting period, it is clear that the month of 'Alá, the month of fasting, comprises the nineteen days preceding the day of Naw-Rúz which is the first day of the month of Bahá of the subsequent Bahá'í year. Adjustments in the length of the year to ensure that Naw-Rúz is on the day of the spring equinox will be made by adding a fifth day to the Ayyám-i-Há, the intercalary days.

The 'Prayer of Fasting' referred to in *Gleanings from the Writings of Bahá'u'lláh*, p. 337, is published in *Tasbíḥ va Tahlíl* (Ṭihrán: Bahá'í Publishing Trust, 129), pp. 64–76. No English translation is available at this time . . .

In the Kitáb-i-Aqdas, Bahá'u'lláh has clearly exempted those who are ill; therefore, you should not feel deprived if you are unable to fast the entire nineteen days. However, there is nothing to prevent a believer from fasting at times other than that prescribed, but it is not a requirement to compensate for days of illness.[3]

As to the question on smoking in relation to the Fast, the Guardian's translation of the passage to which you refer is that one must 'abstain from food and drink' during the hours of fasting. This should be regarded as sufficient guidance for the Western friends for the time being.[4]

It is true that Baha'u'lláh has ordained in the Kitáb-i-Aqdas that in the high latitudes where the duration of days and nights varies considerably clocks should be relied upon rather than the rising and setting of the sun. However, we feel that Dublin is too far south for the application of this law. You should thus judge the end of each day by the actual sunset.[5]

REFLECTIONS ON THE FAST

An Open Letter

To those who are approaching their first Bahá'í Fast

ALTHOUGH fasting is an ancient religious practice, it is seldom done in our culture. Few of us indeed have ever voluntarily gone without food or water for extended periods for any reason, religious or not.

This is an age of instant gratification; self-denial is alien to most people these days.

There is, of course, dieting, but we can stop that at will (or by admitting our weakness), and it leads to results we can measure by stepping on a bathroom scale.

Unlike a diet, fasting is obligatory for a Bahá'í, part of his Covenant with Bahá'u'lláh, and its results are not so easily measured. But like the prayers the Blessed Beauty has revealed for our daily use, it is indispensable to learning to surrender our will to Him.

Faithfully observe it

'In the Prayer of Fasting', Bahá'u'lláh wrote,

We have revealed: 'Should Thy Will decree that out of Thy mouth these words proceed and be addressed unto them, "Observe, for My Beauty's sake, the fast, O people, and set no limit to its duration," I swear by the majesty of Thy glory, that every one of them will faithfully observe it, will abstain from whatsoever will violate Thy law, and will continue to do so until they yield up their souls unto Thee.' In this consisteth the complete surrender of one's will to the Will of God. Meditate on this, that thou mayest drink in the waters of everlasting life which flow through the words of the Lord of all mankind, and mayest testify that the one true God hath ever been immeasurably exalted above His creatures. He, verily, is the Incomparable, the Ever-Abiding, the Omniscient, the All-Wise. (*Gleanings*, p. 337)

Fasting is yet another bounty He has given us to benefit our souls. Neglecting it will surely harm them.

To fast for nineteen days in a row must seem to many new Bahá'ís a pulse-quickening challenge to their self-control and endurance. 'How will I handle it?' you may well ask yourself. 'What if I can't? What if I fail?'

I would like to offer some insights and assurances from one who is approaching his sixteenth fast.

One day at a time

First, I would like to assure you that the fast is not excessively hard. It lasts long enough each day to cause a reasonably noticeable hunger and thirst.

Gently but persistently, that hunger and thirst remind us how frail we are, how vulnerable to the demands of our physical nature.

If we were inclined before the fast to feel strong and independent, our hunger takes us down a peg. We learn that reliance on the necessary things of this world is a weakness we cannot transcend in this life. Yet God teaches this lesson gently and with love.

We say the fast lasts nineteen days; in fact, it lasts only twelve hours each day. Take it one day at a time.

You may find, as I have, that nineteen days is an ideal length of time for the fast. It is long enough to give real spiritual benefit without becoming burdensome.

At first, I have to deliberately break my usual eating

patterns. I have to remember not to drink when I get thirsty. It inconveniences me a little.

As the days pass, though, I cease to focus on the moment-to-moment challenge of fasting and begin to sense the growth in my spirit.

My fasts have generally progressed through an initial stage, when I am consciously adjusting to the unaccustomed abstinence from food and drink, to a stage at which I scarcely feel hunger. In its place, I feel my spirit becoming more susceptible to the influence of God's love and to His presence in my life.

More than once, I've approached the end of a fast wishing I could extend it throughout the year so I could continue to feel the peace, and gain the insights, which it brings to my soul.

'Spiritual lunch'

You may find that you have some extra free time during the fast. Don't forgo breakfast to gain an extra hour or two of sleep in the morning. Your hunger will so distract you it will very likely ruin your day.

Instead, rise joyfully before daybreak and have a hearty breakfast. Then use the time before going to work for prayer, meditation, recitation of the holy verses and deepening.

Devote your lunch time to more prayer and meditation, a 'spiritual lunch', rather than feeling sorry for your stomach. Your stomach will survive, and your spirit will thrive!

The mystical Writings especially yield their greatest treasures to me during the fast. *The Seven Valleys, The Four Valleys, The Hidden Words* and many similar Tablets contain gems of spiritual wisdom that are most accessible in this special month.

If you have found them obscure before, or if you have
been intimidated by their depth, devote some time to
reading and meditating on them now. They have truly
come alive for me during the fast.

Use the prayers for fasting in the back of your prayer
book. They are long, to be sure, but you will have the
time to read them and meditate on their meanings. They
are filled with reminders of the proper attitude to take
when fasting, and of the bounties in store for those who
faithfully observe the fast.

Recite them aloud, for the Blessed Beauty has
promised,

Whoso reciteth in the privacy of his chamber the verses
revealed by God, the scattering angels of the Almighty shall
scatter abroad the fragrance of the words uttered by his
mouth, and shall cause the heart of every righteous man to
throb. Though he may, at first, remain unaware of its effect,
yet the virtue of the grace vouchsafed unto him must needs
sooner or later exercise its influence upon his soul.

An open channel

Although the Christian Church no longer emphasizes
fasting, Jesus offers some advice that is worth recalling:
    'Moreover when ye fast,' He says,

be not, as the hypocrites, of a sad countenance: for they
disfigure their faces, that they may appear unto men to fast.
    Verily I say unto you, They have their reward. But thou,
when thou fastest, anoint thy head, and wash thy face; that
thou appear not unto men to fast, but unto thy Father which
is in secret: and thy Father, which seeth in secret, shall reward
thee openly. (Matt. 6:16–18)

I find that keeping my fast largely a private matter
between God and me opens a channel of constant

communion with Him as I go about my daily business in the fasting period.

Appreciate your hunger and turn it to positive use. Let it prompt you to remember that you are fasting in obedience to God's command, and for love of Him, and 'in complete detachment from all else' but Him.

If you will let your hunger stimulate you to loving remembrance of God, you will achieve a degree of inner peace beyond any other you can find.

Making the effort

Above all, don't become discouraged. You may well find yourself living for six o'clock and the opportunity to break your fast. That is a natural and very human response to fasting.

If that happens, use your period of evening prayer to 'bring thyself to account', meditating on the attitudes that distracted you during the day and resolving to correct them the next day.

Pray for forgiveness, and trust Bahá'u'lláh's promise, 'Whoso maketh efforts for Us, in Our ways will We guide them.'

At the end of the fasting period, if you have sincerely 'made efforts' for God and tried to understand and gain the benefit of the fast, you will find that your soul has undergone a course of therapy.

Like the proverbial mirror turned toward the sun, it will have been polished and adjusted to reflect God's glory, beauty and peace for the new year.[1]

THOMAS F. ARMISTEAD

BAHÁ'U'LLÁH attaches extraordinary importance to the fasting period and the virtues wherewith fasting has been endowed by God from time immemorial – and is re-endowed, so to speak, by Bahá'u'lláh Himself. In one of His Tablets He states that 'the fast . . . enjoined on all' is a particular period during which the servants of God cling to the cord of His commandments and seize upon the handle of His precepts. Addressing God in one of His prayers He writes:

These are the days whereon Thou hast bidden all men to observe the fast, that through it they may purify their souls and rid themselves of all attachment to any one but Thee . . . Grant, O my Lord, that this fast may become a river of life-giving waters and may yield the virtue wherewith Thou hast endowed it. Cleanse Thou by its means the hearts of Thy servants whom the evils of the world have failed to hinder from turning towards Thine all-glorious Name . . .

The fast is amongst Bahá'u'lláh's 'wondrous laws and precepts'; one should fast, He says, for love of God and in pursuance of His injunction, and states 'Blessed is he that observeth the fast wholly for Thy sake', and prays God to assist His servants to 'obey Thee and to keep Thy precepts' and puts this supplication into the mouths of His servants, that this observance of the fast may 'cleanse us from the noisome savours of our trans-gressions, O Thou Who hast called Thyself the God of mercy!' So great, Bahá'u'lláh affirms, is the fast that it adorns the 'preamble of the Book of Thy Laws', and He goes on to say that God has 'endowed every hour of these days with a special virtue . . .'

* * *

The long prayer for the fast grows on one all the adult years of one's life until in the end the blessing of keeping the fast and the blessing of saying this prayer with it become one great annual bounty, one special privilege of life. If one begins at about five minutes before sunrise one discovers that it seems deliberately to be synchronized with the rising of the sun: one finds oneself standing at 'the gate of the city of Thy presence', awaiting God's grace; then come 'the shadow of Thy mercy and the canopy of Thy bounty' – the differentiation of light from dark is taking place, the birds are singing; there follows 'the splendour of Thy luminous brow and the brightness of the light of Thy countenance' – the sky is beginning to kindle with colour; the worshipper asks to be allowed 'to gaze on the Day-Star of Thy Beauty' – the sun is rising! Next comes the full panoply of dawn, symbol of the Divine Springtime of God, 'by the Tabernacle of Thy majesty upon the loftiest summits, and the Canopy of Thy Revelation on the highest hills'; as one gazes upon the sun beginning to mount the skies one reaches the words 'by Thy Beauty that shineth forth above the horizon of eternity, a Beauty before which as soon as it revealeth itself the kingdom of beauty boweth down in worship'. All this takes place in the first half of the prayer. But what the worshipper is supplicating for is: to receive God's grace, to draw nearer to Him, to become attracted to Him and imbibe His words, to serve His Cause in such wise that he may not be held back by those who have turned away from God, to enable him to recognize God's Manifestation, to accomplish what God desires, to grant that 'I may die to all that I possess and live to whatsoever belongeth unto Thee', to remember and praise God, to remove him far from whatever displeases God and enable him to draw near to the One Who manifests God's signs, to make known to this worshipper what was hidden in God's knowledge and

wisdom, to number him with those who have attained
to what God has revealed, to record for him what has
been written down by God for His trusted and chosen
ones, to write down for everyone who has turned unto
God and observed the fast prescribed by Him 'the
recompense decreed for such as speak not except by Thy
leave, and who forsook all that they possessed in Thy
path and for love of Thee', and, last of all, to 'cancel the
trespasses of those who have held fast to Thy laws, and
have observed what Thou hast prescribed unto them in
Thy Book.' Almost like a leitmotiv in a sumptuous
musical composition, there occurs the same refrain over
and over: 'Thou seest me, O my God, holding to Thy
Name, the Most Holy, the Most Luminous, the Most
Mighty, the Most Great, the Most Exalted, the Most
Glorious, and clinging to the hem of the robe to which
have clung all in this world and in the world to come.'
When I repeat this I always visualize myself and my
parents and loved ones who are dead, clinging all
together to this symbolic celestial robe, and I feel very
close to them. Truly a majestic prayer, containing
metaphors of deep mysticism, a prayer that is a never-
ending experience.[2]

'AMATU'L-BAHÁ RUḤIYYIH KHÁNUM

How fitting was the prelude to this year . . . our Fast –
symbolic of the will to sacrifice and wholly yield the self
to God. As we abstained from food and drink, we
became deeply conscious of the things for which He [the
Báb] forfeited His life . . . the cherished hopes of men
for promised peace, and unity of mankind.

He chose our hearts and asked of us surrender of the

ancient hurts, the active fears and failings with which we wound each other and mar the splendid unity we seek in Faith.

Can we find strength and will to cancel out the caustic criticisms, the long-embroidered slights, the outraged pride, the unexplained hostility, the bitterness of ingrown loneliness, the cruel-edged perfection with which we weigh each other? These are the heavy weights which ground our spirits and our prayers.

Then, let us turn our hearts to God and pray with fervour for that sense of love to truly do Him honour, since this alone can change all things and men, because it changes us.[3]

NATIONAL SPIRITUAL ASSEMBLY OF THE BAHÁ'ÍS
OF THE UNITED STATES

MÍRZÁ Abu'l-Faḍl, the great Bahá'í scholar, states that the laws of God in the Holy Books of past religions and those of the *Kitáb-i-Aqdas* may be divided into three categories. The first category is devotional laws and ordinances which concern man's worship of God. The ordinances of obligatory prayer, fasting and similar devotional acts are among this group of laws.

The second category is laws which benefit the individual only, such as cleanliness and other acts which are aimed at elevating the personal and spiritual condition of the individual.

The third category is the laws which concern society . . .[4]

ADIB TAHERZADEH

As for fasting, its effects are even more clear and manifest, more perfect and exalted [than religious donations]. For fasting possesses all the benefits of prayer . . . while it also effectively disciplines the animal self and curbs the defiance of the appetitive faculties. This is obvious for all to see, and it does not require lengthy discourse or excessive explanation. For it is evident that man is one of the animal species, and animal faculties are intrinsically attracted to the natures imprinted on them and inclined to the pleasures derived from their disposition. We have explained in our other works that the legislative faculty, be it divine or human, belongs to the natural faculties and regulates the deeds that issue from the lower self. For it is impossible to restrain the wilfulness of the self and turn it away from base pleasures and destructive, animal desires save by training it with the discipline of the Divine Law which has been handed down, and withholding it from grave offences by means of prescribed moral standards. This should not be through arduous, artificial restraint, as the Sufis believe, or solely through refinement and learning in schools, as naturalist philosophers maintain.[5]

MÍRZÁ ABU'L-FAḌL

KNOW thou that Fasting is a command given in all the Holy Books in all times. The outward appearance thereof is restraining the self from that which is prohibited in the Books.

Special times are appointed and particular forms are ordained by every religion. The Zoroastrians have certain forms, the Jews have others; the Christians, the Muhammadans, each differ in their forms, and the Bahá'ís have forms of fasting differing from all former religions. These apparent or outward differences were according to the exigencies of the times when given.

The outward fruit of fasting is the preservation of the material health through the purifying of the body once a year. The inward fruits pertain to the other states of existence.

In the world of *soul* its fruit is the sanctifying of the soul from the animal qualities and clothing it with the intellectual attributes, thereby releasing the soul from the lower human nature.

In the world of *mind*, it is the process of filtering, sifting out the dust and taints and dross of the self, and soaring to the Spiritual and Divine Kingdoms.

In the world of *spirit*, it is the longing, the aspiring to the stations of Divinity, and attaining to the meeting of God in both this world and those to come after death.

Thus one of the doors, through which one may attain to the meeting of God and entrance into His Kingdom, is fasting; *but success depends upon following the forms prescribed in the Heavenly Book.*

* * *

Another important point is this: Whoever, in this day, is firm and steadfast in the Covenant of the Blessed Perfection and keeps himself from turning to aught else save the Centre of His Covenant, 'Abdu'l-Bahá, is of those who fast. Therefore, it is incumbent that man shall adorn himself with the attributes of his highness, 'Abdu'l-Bahá, and shall follow His example in dealing with the people of the world. He must consider the benefits of others rather than his own. He must consider the promotion of the Word of God, and the spreading of His Fragrances, even as the material gain of business, the cause of wealth and the capital of his prosperity.

* * *

Nothing, after prayer, will cause the development of the spirit, save fasting. The Primal Point, the Báb, ordained for all the people to fast until they should reach the age of forty-two, but the Blessed Perfection said: 'We love fasting! Unless the people become old and weak, they should fast.' Thus the limit for fasting was appointed. One should begin to observe the fast from the age of fifteen, and continue the observance of it until the body may become too weak to do so without injury. His Holiness, the Blessed Perfection, used to fast throughout the set time every year . . .

* * *

In Mark 9:7–29, is related the story of the afflicted child who was brought to Jesus by the disciples after their vain efforts to cast out from him the spirit which tormented him and of his being healed by Jesus, who said, in reply to a question from the disciples, that: 'This kind can come forth by nothing but by prayer and fasting.'

Thus Jesus taught that fasting and praying give strength to the spirit of man, so that it may become enabled to heal the different violent and strong sicknesses which possess him.

* * *

The results and fruits of these acts are innumerable, but the few that have been mentioned are the principal ones. We ask the Merciful Lord that this blessed act may become a cause of quenching the fires of lustfulness, animosity and hatred.[6]

MÍRZÁ ASADU'LLÁH-I-IṢFAHÁNÍ

As the month of the fast ends at the March equinox, the fast always falls in the same season, namely, spring in the Northern, and autumn in the Southern, Hemisphere; never in the extreme heat of summer nor in the extreme cold of winter, when hardship would be likely to result. At that season, moreover, the interval between sunrise and sunset is approximately the same all over the habitable portion of the globe, namely, from about 6 A.M. to 6 P.M. The fast is not binding on children and invalids, on travellers, or on those who are too old or too weak (including women who are with child or have babes at the breast).

There is much evidence to show that a periodical fast such as is enjoined by the Bahá'í teachings is beneficial as a measure of physical hygiene, but just as the reality of the Bahá'í feast does not lie in the consumption of physical food, but in the commemoration of God, which is our spiritual food, so the reality of the Bahá'í fast does not consist in abstention from physical food, although that may help in the purification of the body, but in the abstention from the desires and lusts of the flesh, and in severance from all save God.[7]

J. E. ESSLEMONT

FIRMNESS in the Covenant will cement the marriage bond, unite families, and draw together all factions, groups and classes.

The believer in his efforts to carry out his Bahá'í responsibilities will encounter difficulties, obstacles and opposition on all sides, and frequently, many of these troubles will arise from those nearest to him.

This opposition is to be expected, for trouble is

inherent in this earthly existence, and no one is exempt therefrom . . .

One way to safeguard Bahá'í rights is to have a complete understanding with . . . non-Bahá'í relatives regarding this matter. In this way the believer can protect his Covenant with God. In this sacred matter, hesitancy or timidity should not deter the believer from asking for the necessary time to fulfil his spiritual obligations. Time should be provided for meetings, the Nineteen-Day Feasts, Holy Days and anniversaries. The nineteen-day Fast should be explained. In this respect the believer is not asking for more than he would require as an active member of any religious body. In both cases, time, effort and finances are necessary.[8]

M. SETO

THE period of fasting ordained by Bahá'u'lláh is among his laws for the spiritual regeneration of mankind. Its purpose is not that His servants should go hungry, but that they should learn detachment from this physical world and the appetites of self. In the prayers revealed for the fasting period, He asks that the Fast 'cleanse . . . the hearts of Thy servants' and that those who keep the Fast may 'detach themselves entirely from all except Thyself'. He warns His followers to 'beware lest desire deprive you of this grace that is appointed in the Book'. The Fast is for our benefit, but we will not receive its bounties if we do not control our physical desires.

In a Tablet to an individual (see pp. 6–7 above) Bahá'u'lláh illustrates the depth to which we should detach ourselves from our personal, physical, selfish desires. He says that if He were to ordain that the people should fast and no time were to be given to stop fasting, all would continue fasting until they had given their souls back to God. This is the ultimate in detachment: complete surrender to the Will of God to the extent that our own lives would mean nothing.

He did not ask us to fast to such an extreme, but that is the level of detachment for which we should aim. In the prayers for the Fast, Bahá'u'lláh repeatedly stresses this point by stating that we are to die to all we possess and live to whatever is God's. His prayer for those who fast is 'that they may purify their souls and rid themselves of all attachment to anyone but Thee', and 'blessed is he that observeth the fast wholly for Thy sake and with absolute detachment from all things except Thee'. He prays, too, that the Fast may become a river of life-giving waters for our souls.

All this is possible, and especially possible during the time Bahá'u'lláh has set aside for the Fast, for He affirms to God that 'Thou hast endowed every hour of these days with a special virtue inscrutable to all except Thee'. We cannot know the power invested in these days of fasting, but we can be assured that they are special days indeed. They are the days when we ask God to 'enable us to soar in the heavens of Thy transcendent glory'. To do this we have to remove ourselves from all that is contrary to God's Will; for this we detach ourselves from the physical world.

'Abdu'l-Bahá says that we should fast because the Messengers of God have fasted. When revealing their teachings and establishing their laws, the Manifestations fasted. Every sincere soul who loves someone longs to experience what that loved one has experienced; therefore, since the Prophets fasted, we too should fast – if for no other reason. They fasted when revealing Their teachings and establishing Their laws; our fasting

indicates faithfulness to those teachings and obedience
to those laws.

'Abdu'l-Bahá also explained that fasting (together
with prayer) is a cause of 'awakening and mindfulness',
and is conducive to 'protection and preservation from
tests'. Our senses are sharpened and we become more
open to spiritual impulses. At the same time our reliance
on our physical (or animal) impulses is lessened. Our
identity as spiritual beings is intensified. This break in
daily routine allows us the concentrated opportunity to
realign our outward actions with our inner nature.
Mindful of our spiritual essence, we turn our attention
to our heavenly virtues and are less influenced by our
animalistic urges, and so we are protected from acts not
conducive to our well-being.

And fasting is symbolic. Our lives are to be examples
of detachment and self-restraint – and fasting is a
symbol of that. As spiritual beings we are not bound by
the appetites of our physical selves. We gain mastery
and control over them in order to take on the
characteristics of the spirit, to be carried away by the
breathings of heaven and to catch fire from the love of
God. As we do so we become more perfect spiritual
beings.

Material fasting is a token of our spiritual detachment. The physical fast is simply restraint from eating
physical food: physical detachment. The greater detachment is the spiritual fast: detachment from all desires of
the self. This latter is our goal and the harder to attain.
Still, we have the material fast to remind us and help us
on our way towards real detachment.

The Guardian assures us that prayer and fasting will
help us in this struggle. He said they 'act as stimulants to
the soul, strengthen, revive and purify it, and thus
ensure its steady development'. The fasting time, he

said, is 'essentially a period of meditation and prayer, of spiritual recuperation'. He did not say it was a time of hunger, so the incidental hunger is of no consequence. It is not important. The significance and purpose of the fast is 'fundamentally spiritual in character'.

Yet what about the person who, for medical reasons, cannot observe the physical fast? Will that individual be denied spiritual development because the body is incapable of sustaining that length of time without certain nutrients? Is the will of God capricious? Is that person to be deprived of the benefits and bounties of fasting?

Not necessarily. In the prayer of Naw-Rúz, at the close of the Fast, Bahá'u'lláh proclaims: 'Shouldst Thou regard him who hath broken the fast as one who hath observed it, such a man would be reckoned among them who from eternity had been keeping the fast. And shouldst Thou decree that he who hath observed the fast hath broken it that person would be . . . far removed from the crystal waters of this living Fountain.' At that distance, the soul is not likely to receive much relief from the spiritual desert.

Clearly the eating (or not eating) of food is not the most important aspect of observing the Fast. If the doctor says you should not fast, or if any of the other conditions apply which Bahá'u'lláh says will exempt you – you should not. It is not our actions that determine the grace of God, but our motives. Less than perfect actions can be accepted, and therefore perfected, by Bahá'u'lláh if our hearts are pure and our motives spotless. The purpose of the Fast remains: spiritual recuperation, in the words of the Guardian; self-restraint, in the words of 'Abdu'l-Bahá; and detachment, in the words of Bahá'u'lláh. This is the significance of the Fast.

If a person cannot observe the physical side of the Fast there is no reason for him to ignore the reality of it. If we do not concern ourselves with the essence of the Fast, then are we not like those who, Bahá'u'lláh says, 'have fasted in the daytime . . . and who have repudiated Thy truth, disbelieved in Thy signs, gainsaid Thy testimony, and perverted Thine utterances'? It is not just by our actions (not eating) that we observe the Fast. We have to observe it with our hearts. And it may be an even greater challenge for those individuals who cannot keep the physical Fast, to satisfy their body's special requirements *while at the same time* seeking that level of detachment and spiritual readjustment which is the purpose of the Fast.

To aid and assist us Bahá'u'lláh has revealed special prayers for this time of fasting. They help focus our hearts and minds on the spiritual reality of these special days. Therefore even if we have to eat for medical reasons, we can observe the Fast, its intent and essence, in our hearts and prayers.9

DUANE L. HERRMANN

PRAYERS FOR THE FAST

I

I BESEECH Thee, O my God,
  by Thy mighty Sign,
and by the revelation of Thy grace amongst men,
  to cast me not away
from the gate of the city of Thy presence,
  and to disappoint not the hopes I have set
on the manifestations of Thy grace
  amidst Thy creatures.
Thou seest me, O my God,
  holding to Thy Name,
    the Most Holy,
      the Most Luminous,
        the Most Mighty,
          the Most Great,
            the Most Exalted,
              the Most Glorious,
and clinging to the hem of the robe
  to which have clung
all in this world and in the world to come.

I beseech Thee, O my God,
  by Thy most sweet Voice and by Thy most exalted
    Word,
to draw me ever nearer to the threshold of Thy door,
  and to suffer me not
to be far removed from the shadow of Thy mercy
  and the canopy of Thy bounty.
Thou seest me, O my God,
  holding to Thy Name,

the Most Holy,
　　the Most Luminous,
　　　the Most Mighty,
　　　　the Most Great,
　　　　　the Most Exalted,
　　　　　　the Most Glorious,
and clinging to the hem of the robe
　　to which have clung
all in this world and in the world to come.

I beseech Thee, O my God,
　　by the splendour of Thy luminous brow
and the brightness of the light of Thy countenance,
　　which shineth from the all-highest horizon,
to attract me
　　by the fragrance of Thy raiment,
and make me drink
　　of the choice wine of Thine utterance.
Thou seest me, O my God,
　　holding to Thy Name,
　　　the Most Holy,
　　　　the Most Luminous,
　　　　　the Most Mighty,
　　　　　　the Most Great,
　　　　　　　the Most Exalted,
　　　　　　　　the Most Glorious,
and clinging to the hem of the robe
　　to which have clung
all in this world and in the world to come.

I beseech Thee, O my God,
　　by Thy hair which moveth across Thy face,
even as Thy most exalted pen
　　moveth across the pages of Thy Tablets,
shedding the musk of hidden meanings

over the kingdom of Thy creation,
so to raise me up to serve Thy Cause
   that I shall not fall back,
nor be hindered
   by the suggestions of them
who have cavilled at Thy signs
   and turned away from Thy face.
Thou seest me, O my God,
   holding to Thy Name,
     the Most Holy,
       the Most Luminous,
        the Most Mighty,
         the Most Great,
          the Most Exalted,
           the Most Glorious,
and clinging to the hem of the robe
   to which have clung
all in this world and in the world to come.

I beseech Thee, O my God,
   by Thy Name
which Thou has made the King of Names,
   by which all who are in heaven
and all who are on earth
   have been enraptured,
to enable me to gaze
   on the Day-Star of Thy Beauty,
and to supply me with the wine of Thine utterance.
Thou seest me, O my God,
   holding to Thy Name,
     the Most Holy,
       the Most Luminous,
        the Most Mighty,
         the Most Great,
          the Most Exalted,

the Most Glorious,
and clinging to the hem of the robe
    to which have clung
all in this world and in the world to come.

I beseech Thee, O my God,
    by the Tabernacle of Thy majesty
upon the loftiest summits,
    and the Canopy of Thy Revelation
on the highest hills,
    to graciously aid me
to do what Thy will hath desired
    and Thy purpose hath manifested.
Thou seest me, O my God,
    holding to Thy Name,
        the Most Holy,
            the Most Luminous,
                the Most Mighty,
                    the Most Great,
                        the Most Exalted,
                            the Most Glorious,
and clinging to the hem of the robe
    to which have clung
all in this world and in the world to come.

I beseech Thee, O my God,
    by Thy Beauty that shineth forth
above the horizon of eternity,
    a Beauty before which
as soon as it revealeth itself
    the kingdom of beauty boweth down in worship,
magnifying it in ringing tones,
    to grant that I may die to all that I possess,
and live to whatsoever
    belongeth unto Thee.

Thou seest me, O my God,
  holding to Thy Name,
    the Most Holy,
      the Most Luminous,
        the Most Mighty,
          the Most Great,
            the Most Exalted,
              the Most Glorious,
and clinging to the hem of the robe
  to which have clung
all in this world and in the world to come.

I beseech Thee, O my God,
  by the Manifestation of Thy Name,
the Well-Beloved,
    through Whom the hearts of Thy lovers were
      consumed
and the souls of all that dwell on earth
  have soared aloft,
to aid me to remember Thee amongst Thy creatures,
  and to extol Thee amidst Thy people.
Thou seest me, O my God,
  holding to Thy Name,
    the Most Holy,
      the Most Luminous,
        the Most Mighty,
          the Most Great,
            the Most Exalted,
              the Most Glorious,
and clinging to the hem of the robe
  to which have clung
all in this world and in the world to come.

I beseech Thee, O my God,
  by the rustling of the Divine Lote-Tree

and the murmur of the breezes of Thine utterance
    in the kingdom of Thy names,
to remove me far from
    whatsoever Thy will abhorreth,
and draw me nigh
    unto the station
wherein He Who is the Day-Spring of Thy signs
    hath shone forth.
Thou seest me, O my God,
    holding to Thy Name,
      the Most Holy,
        the Most Luminous,
          the Most Mighty,
            the Most Great,
              the Most Exalted,
                the Most Glorious,
and clinging to the hem of the robe
    to which have clung
all in this world and in the world to come.

I beseech Thee, O my God,
    by that Letter, which
as soon as it proceeded
    out of the mouth of Thy will,
hath caused the oceans to surge,
    and the winds to blow,
and the fruits to be revealed,
    and the trees to spring forth,
and all past traces to vanish,
    and all veils to be rent asunder,
and them who are devoted to Thee to hasten
    unto the light of the countenance of their Lord,
the Unconstrained,
    to make known unto me

what lay hid in the treasuries of Thy knowledge
   and concealed within the repositories of Thy wisdom.
Thou seest me, O my God,
   holding to Thy Name,
     the Most Holy,
       the Most Luminous,
        the Most Mighty,
         the Most Great,
          the Most Exalted,
           the Most Glorious,
and clinging to the hem of the robe
   to which have clung
all in this world and in the world to come.

I beseech Thee, O my God,
   by the fire of Thy love
which drove sleep from the eyes of Thy chosen ones
   and Thy loved ones,
and by their remembrance and praise of Thee
   at the hour of dawn,
to number me
   with such as have attained
unto that which Thou hast sent down in Thy Book
   and manifested through Thy will.
Thou seest me, O my God,
   holding to Thy Name,
     the Most Holy,
       the Most Luminous,
        the Most Mighty,
         the Most Great,
          the Most Exalted,
           the Most Glorious,
and clinging to the hem of the robe
   to which have clung
all in this world and in the world to come.

I beseech Thee, O my God,
   by the light of Thy countenance
which impelled them who are nigh unto Thee
   to meet the darts of Thy decree,
and such as are devoted to Thee
   to face the swords of Thine enemies in Thy path,
to write down for me
   with Thy most exalted Pen
what Thou hast written down for Thy trusted ones
   and Thy chosen ones.
Thou seest me, O my God,
   holding to Thy Name,
      the Most Holy,
         the Most Luminous,
            the Most Mighty,
               the Most Great,
                  the Most Exalted,
                     the Most Glorious,
and clinging to the hem of the robe
   to which have clung
all in this world and in the world to come.

I beseech Thee, O my God,
   by Thy Name through which
Thou hast hearkened unto the call of Thy lovers,
   and the sighs of them that long for Thee,
and the cry of them that enjoy near access to Thee,
   and the groaning of them that are devoted to Thee,
and through which Thou hast fulfilled the wishes
   of them that have set their hopes on Thee,
and hast granted them their desires,
   through Thy grace and Thy favours,
      and by Thy Name
      through which
the ocean of forgiveness

surged before Thy face,
and the clouds of Thy generosity
   rained upon Thy servants,
to write down for every one
   who hath turned unto Thee,
and observed the fast prescribed by Thee,
   the recompense decreed
for such as speak not except by Thy leave,
   and who forsook all that they possessed
     in Thy path
     and for love of Thee.

I beseech Thee, O my Lord,
   by Thyself, and by Thy signs,
and Thy clear tokens, and the shining light
   of the Day-Star of Thy Beauty,
and Thy Branches,
   to cancel the trespasses of those
who have held fast to Thy laws, and have observed
   what Thou hast prescribed unto them in Thy Book.
Thou seest me, O my God,
   holding to Thy Name,
     the Most Holy,
       the Most Luminous,
         the Most Mighty,
           the Most Great,
             the Most Exalted,
               the Most Glorious,
and clinging to the hem of the robe
   to which have clung
all in this world and in the world to come.

BAHÁ'U'LLÁH

2

THESE are, O my God, the days whereon Thou didst
enjoin Thy servants to observe the fast. With it Thou
didst adorn the preamble of the Book of Thy Laws
revealed unto Thy creatures, and didst deck forth the
Repositories of Thy commandments in the sight of all
who are in Thy heaven and all who are on Thy earth.
Thou hast endowed every hour of these days with a
special virtue, inscrutable to all except Thee, Whose
knowledge embraceth all created things. Thou hast,
also, assigned unto every soul a portion of this virtue in
accordance with the Tablet of Thy decree and the
Scriptures of Thine irrevocable judgment. Every leaf of
these Books and Scriptures Thou hast, moreover,
allotted to each one of the peoples and kindreds of the
earth.

For Thine ardent lovers Thou hast, according to Thy
decree, reserved, at each daybreak, the cup of Thy
remembrance, O Thou Who art the Ruler of rulers!
These are they who have been so inebriated with the
wine of Thy manifold wisdom that they forsake their
couches in their longing to celebrate Thy praise and
extol Thy virtues, and flee from sleep in their eagerness
to approach Thy presence and partake of Thy bounty.
Their eyes have, at all times, been bent upon the Day-
Spring of Thy loving-kindness, and their faces set
towards the Fountain-Head of Thine inspiration. Rain
down, then, upon us and upon them from the clouds of
Thy mercy what beseemeth the heaven of Thy bounteousness and grace.

Lauded be Thy name, O my God! This is the hour
when Thou hast unlocked the doors of Thy bounty
before the faces of Thy creatures, and opened wide the
portals of Thy tender mercy unto all the dwellers of

Thine earth. I beseech Thee, by all them whose blood was shed in Thy path, who, in their yearning over Thee, rid themselves from all attachment to any of Thy creatures, and who were so carried away by the sweet savours of Thine inspiration that every single member of their bodies intoned Thy praise and vibrated to Thy remembrance, not to withhold from us the things Thou hast irrevocably ordained in this Revelation – a Revelation the potency of which hath caused every tree to cry out what the Burning Bush had aforetime proclaimed unto Moses, Who conversed with Thee, a Revelation that hath enabled every least pebble to resound again with Thy praise, as the stones glorified Thee in the days of Muḥammad, Thy Friend.

These are the ones, O my God, whom Thou hast graciously enabled to have fellowship with Thee and to commune with Him Who is the Revealer of Thyself. The winds of Thy will have scattered them abroad until Thou didst gather them together beneath Thy shadow, and didst cause them to enter into the precincts of Thy court. Now that Thou hast made them to abide under the shade of the canopy of Thy mercy, do Thou assist them to attain what must befit so august a station. Suffer them not, O my Lord, to be numbered with them who, though enjoying near access to Thee, have been kept back from recognizing Thy face, and who, though meeting with Thee, are deprived of Thy presence.

These are Thy servants, O my Lord, who have entered with Thee in this, the Most Great Prison, who have kept the fast within its walls according to what Thou hadst commanded them in the Tablets of Thy decree and the Books of Thy behest. Send down, therefore, upon them what will thoroughly purge them of all Thou abhorrest, that they may be wholly devoted to Thee, and may detach themselves entirely from all except Thyself.

Rain down, then, upon us, O my God, that which beseemeth Thy grace and befitteth Thy bounty. Enable us, then, O my God, to live in remembrance of Thee and to die in love of Thee, and supply us with the gift of Thy presence in Thy worlds hereafter – worlds which are inscrutable to all except Thee. Thou art our Lord and the Lord of all worlds, and the God of all that are in heaven and all that are on earth.

Thou beholdest, O my God, what hath befallen Thy dear ones in Thy days. Thy glory beareth me witness! The voice of the lamentation of Thy chosen ones hath been lifted up throughout Thy realm. Some were ensnared by the infidels in Thy land, and were hindered by them from having near access to Thee and from attaining the court of Thy glory. Others were able to approach Thee, but were kept back from beholding Thy face. Still others were permitted, in their eagerness to look upon Thee, to enter the precincts of Thy court, but they allowed the veils of the imaginations of Thy creatures and the wrongs inflicted by the oppressors among Thy people to come in between them and Thee.

This is the hour, O my Lord, which Thou hast caused to excel every other hour, and hast related it to the choicest among Thy creatures. I beseech Thee, O my God, by Thy Self and by them, to ordain in the course of this year what shall exalt Thy loved ones. Do Thou, moreover, decree within this year what will enable the Day-Star of Thy power to shine brightly above the horizon of Thy glory, and to illuminate, by Thy sovereign might, the whole world.

Render Thy Cause victorious, O my Lord, and abase Thou Thine enemies. Write down, then, for us the good of this life and of the life to come. Thou art the Truth,

Who knoweth the secret things. No God is there but Thee, the Ever-Forgiving, the All-Bountiful.

BaHÁ'U'LLÁH

3

PRAISE be to Thee, O Lord my God! I beseech Thee by this Revelation whereby darkness hath been turned into light, through which the Frequented Fane hath been built, and the Written Tablet revealed, and the Outspread Roll uncovered, to send down upon me and upon them who are in my company that which will enable us to soar into the heavens of Thy transcendent glory, and will wash us from the stain of such doubts as have hindered the suspicious from entering into the tabernacle of Thy unity.

I am the one, O my Lord, who hath held fast the cord of Thy loving-kindness, and clung to the hem of Thy mercy and favours. Do Thou ordain for me and for my loved ones the good of this world and of the world to come. Supply them, then, with the Hidden Gift Thou didst ordain for the choicest among Thy creatures.

These are, O my Lord, the days in which Thou hast bidden Thy servants to observe the fast. Blessed is he that observeth the fast wholly for Thy sake and with absolute detachment from all things except Thee. Assist me and assist them, O my Lord, to obey Thee and to keep Thy precepts. Thou, verily, hast power to do what Thou choosest.

There is no God but Thee, the All-Knowing, the All-Wise. All praise be to God, the Lord of all worlds.

BaHÁ'U'LLÁH

4

GLORY be to Thee, O Lord my God! These are the days whereon Thou hast bidden all men to observe the fast, that through it they may purify their souls and rid themselves of all attachment to any one but Thee, and that out of their hearts may ascend that which will be worthy of the court of Thy majesty and may well beseem the seat of the revelation of Thy oneness. Grant, O my Lord, that this fast may become a river of life-giving waters and may yield the virtue wherewith Thou hast endowed it. Cleanse Thou by its means the hearts of Thy servants whom the evils of the world have failed to hinder from turning towards Thine all-glorious Name, and who have remained unmoved by the noise and tumult of such as have repudiated Thy most resplendent signs which have accompanied the advent of Thy Manifestation Whom Thou hast invested with Thy sovereignty, Thy power, Thy majesty and glory. These are the servants who, as soon as Thy call reached them, hastened in the direction of Thy mercy and were not kept back from Thee by the changes and chances of this world or by any human limitations.

I am he, O my God, who testifieth to Thy unity, who acknowledgeth Thy oneness, who boweth humbly before the revelations of Thy majesty, and who recog-nizeth with downcast countenance the splendours of the light of Thy transcendent glory. I have believed in Thee after Thou didst enable me to know Thy Self, Whom Thou hast revealed to men's eyes through the power of Thy sovereignty and might. Unto Him I have turned, wholly detached from all things, and cleaving stead-fastly unto the cord of Thy gifts and favours. I have embraced His truth, and the truth of all the wondrous laws and precepts that have been sent down unto Him. I have fasted for love of Thee and in pursuance of Thine injunction, and have broken my fast with Thy praise on my tongue and in conformity with Thy pleasure. Suffer me not, O my Lord, to be reckoned among them who have fasted in the daytime, who in the night-season have prostrated themselves before Thy face, and who have repudiated Thy truth, disbelieved in Thy signs, gainsaid Thy testimony, and perverted Thine utterances.

Open Thou, O my Lord, mine eyes and the eyes of all them that have sought Thee, that we may recognize Thee with Thine own eyes. This is Thy bidding given us in the Book sent down by Thee unto Him Who Thou hast chosen by Thy behest, Whom Thou hast singled out for Thy favour above all Thy creatures, Whom Thou hast been pleased to invest with Thy sovereignty, and Whom Thou hast specially favoured and entrusted with Thy Message unto Thy people. Praised be Thou, therefore, O my God, inasmuch as Thou hast graciously enabled us to recognize Him and to acknowledge whatsoever hath been sent down unto Him, and conferred upon us the honour of attaining the presence of the One Whom Thou didst promise in Thy Book and in Thy Tablets.

Thou seest me then, O my God, with my face turned towards Thee, cleaving steadfastly to the cord of Thy gracious providence and generosity, and clinging to the hem of Thy tender mercies and bountiful favours. Destroy not, I implore Thee, my hopes of attaining unto that which Thou didst ordain for Thy servants who have turned towards the precincts of Thy court and the sanctuary of Thy presence, and have observed the fast for love of Thee. I confess, O my God, that whatever proceedeth from me is wholly unworthy of Thy sovereignty and falleth short of Thy majesty. And yet I beseech Thee by Thy Name through which Thou hast revealed Thy Self, in the glory of Thy most excellent titles, unto all created things, in this Revelation whereby Thou hast, through Thy most resplendent Name, manifested Thy beauty, to give me to drink of the wine of Thy mercy and of the pure beverage of Thy favour, which have streamed forth from the right hand of Thy will, that I may so fix my gaze upon Thee and be so detached from all else but Thee, that the world and all that hath been created therein may appear before me as a fleeting day which Thou hast not deigned to create.

I moreover entreat Thee, O my God, to rain down, from the heaven of Thy will and the clouds of Thy mercy, that which will cleanse us from the noisome savours of our transgressions, O Thou Who hast called Thyself the God of Mercy! Thou art, verily, the Most Powerful, the All-Glorious, the Beneficent.

Cast not away, O my Lord, him that hath turned towards Thee, nor suffer him who hath drawn nigh unto Thee to be removed far from Thy court. Dash not the hopes of the suppliant who hath longingly stretched out his hands to seek Thy grace and favours, and deprive not Thy sincere servants of the wonders of Thy tender mercies and loving-kindness. Forgiving and Most Bountiful art Thou, O my Lord! Power hast Thou to do what Thou pleasest. All else but Thee are impotent before the revelations of Thy might, are as lost in the face of the evidences of Thy wealth, are as nothing when compared with the manifestations of Thy transcendent sovereignty, and are destitute of all strength when face to face with the signs and tokens of Thy power. What refuge is there beside Thee, O my Lord, to which I can flee, and where is there a haven to which I can hasten? Nay, the power of Thy might beareth me witness! No protector is there but Thee; no place to flee to except Thee, no refuge to seek save Thee. Cause me to taste, O my Lord, the divine sweetness of Thy remembrance and praise. I swear by Thy might! Whosoever tasteth of its sweetness will rid himself of all attachment to the world and all that is therein, and will set his face towards Thee, cleansed from the remembrance of any one except Thee.

Inspire then my soul, O my God, with Thy wondrous remembrance, that I may glorify Thy name. Number me not with them who read Thy words and fail to find Thy hidden gift which, as decreed by Thee, is contained therein, and which quickeneth the souls of Thy creatures and the hearts of Thy servants. Cause me, O my Lord, to be reckoned among them who have been so stirred up by the sweet savours that have been wafted in Thy days that they have laid down their lives for Thee and hastened to the scene of their death in their longing to gaze on Thy beauty and in their yearning to attain Thy presence. And were any one to say unto them on their way, 'Whither go ye?' they would say, 'Unto God, the All-Possessing, the Help in Peril, the Self-Subsisting!'

The transgressions committed by such as have turned away from Thee and have borne themselves haughtily towards Thee have not availed to hinder them from loving Thee, and from setting their faces towards Thee, and from turning in the direction of Thy mercy. These are they who are blessed by the Concourse on high, who are glorified by the denizens of the everlasting Cities, and beyond them by those on whose foreheads Thy most exalted pen hath written: 'These! The people of Bahá. Through them have been shed the splendours of the light of guidance.' Thus hath it been ordained, at Thy behest and by Thy will, in the Tablet of Thine irrevocable decree.

Proclaim, therefore, O my God, their greatness and

the greatness of those who while living or after death
have circled round them. Supply them with that which
Thou hast ordained for the righteous among Thy
creatures. Potent art Thou to do all things. There is no
God but Thee, the All-Powerful, the Help in Peril, the
Almighty, the Most Bountiful.

Do not bring our fasts to an end with this fast, O my
Lord, nor the covenants Thou hast made with this
covenant. Do Thou accept all that we have done for
love of Thee, and for the sake of Thy pleasure, and all
that we have left undone as a result of our subjection to
our evil and corrupt desires. Enable us, then, to cleave
steadfastly to Thy love and Thy good-pleasure, and
preserve us from the mischief of such as have denied
Thee and repudiated Thy most resplendent signs. Thou
art, in truth, the Lord of this world and of the next. No
God is there beside Thee, the Exalted, the Most High.

Magnify Thou, O Lord my God, Him Who is the
Primal Point, the Divine Mystery, the Unseen Essence,
the Day-Spring of Divinity, and the Manifestation of
Thy Lordship, through Whom all the knowledge of the
past and all the knowledge of the future were made
plain, through Whom the pearls of Thy hidden wisdom
were uncovered, and the mystery of Thy treasured
name disclosed, Whom Thou hast appointed as the
Announcer of the One through Whose name the letter B
and the letter E have been joined and united, through
Whom Thy majesty, Thy sovereignty and Thy might
were made known, through Whom Thy words have
been sent down, and Thy laws set forth with clearness,
and Thy signs spread abroad, and Thy Word established, through Whom the hearts of Thy chosen ones
were laid bare, and all that were in the heavens and all
that were on the earth were gathered together, Whom
Thou hast called 'Alí-Muḥammad in the kingdom of

Thy names, and the Spirit of Spirits in the Tablets of Thine irrevocable decree, Whom Thou hast invested with Thine own title, unto Whose name all other names have, at Thy bidding and through the power of Thy might, been made to return, and in Whom Thou hast caused all Thine attributes and titles to attain their final consummation. To Him also belong such names as lay hid within Thy stainless tabernacles, in Thine invisible world and Thy sanctified cities.

Magnify Thou, moreover, such as have believed in Him and in His signs and have turned towards Him, from among those that have acknowledged Thy unity in His Latter Manifestation – a Manifestation whereof He hath made mention in His Tablets, and in His Books, and in His Scriptures, and in all the wondrous verses and gem-like utterances that have descended upon Him. It is this same Manifestation Whose covenant Thou hast bidden Him establish ere He had established His own covenant. He it is Whose praise the Bayán hath celebrated. In it His excellence hath been extolled, and His truth established, and His sovereignty proclaimed, and His Cause perfected. Blessed is the man that hath turned unto Him, and fulfilled the things He hath commanded, O Thou Who art the Lord of the worlds and the Desire of all them that have known Thee!

Praised be Thou, O my God, inasmuch as Thou hast aided us to recognize and love Him. I, therefore, beseech Thee by Him and by Them Who are the Day-Springs of Thy Divinity, and the Manifestations of Thy Lordship, and the Treasuries of Thy Revelation, and the Depositories of Thine inspiration, to enable us to serve and obey Him, and to empower us to become the helpers of His Cause and the dispersers of His adversaries. Powerful art Thou to do all that pleaseth Thee.

No God is there beside Thee, the Almighty, the All-Glorious, the One Whose help is sought by all men!

BAHÁ'U'LLÁH

5

THOU seest, O God of Mercy, Thou Whose power pervadeth all created things, these servants of Thine, Thy thralls, who, according to the good-pleasure of Thy Will, observe in the daytime the fast prescribed by Thee, who arise, at the earliest dawn of day, to make mention of Thy Name, and to celebrate Thy praise, in the hope of obtaining their share of the goodly things that are treasured up within the treasuries of Thy grace and bounty. I beseech Thee, O Thou that holdest in Thine hands the reins of the entire creation, in Whose grasp is the whole kingdom of Thy names and of Thine attributes, not to deprive, in Thy Day, Thy servants from the showers pouring from the clouds of Thy mercy, nor to hinder them from taking their portion of the ocean of Thy good-pleasure.

All the atoms of the earth bear witness, O my Lord, to the greatness of Thy power and of Thy sovereignty; and all the signs of the universe attest the glory of Thy majesty and of Thy might. Have mercy, then, O Thou Who art the sovereign Lord of all, Who art the King of everlasting days, and Ruler of all nations, upon these Thy servants, who have clung to the cord of Thy commandments, who have bowed their necks to the revelations of Thy laws which have been sent down from the heaven of Thy Will.

Behold, O my Lord, how their eyes are lifted up

towards the dawning-place of Thy loving-kindness, how their hearts are set upon the oceans of Thy favours, how their voices are lowered before the accents of Thy most sweet Voice, calling, from the most sublime Station, in Thy name the All-Glorious. Help Thou Thy loved ones, O my Lord, them that have forsaken their all, that they may obtain the things Thou dost possess, whom trials and tribulations have encompassed for having renounced the world and set their affections on Thy realm of glory. Shield them, I entreat Thee, O my Lord, from the assaults of their evil passions and desires, and aid them to obtain the things that shall profit them in this present world and in the next.

I pray Thee, O my Lord, by Thy hidden, Thy treasured Name, that calleth aloud in the kingdom of creation, and summoneth all peoples to the Tree beyond which there is no passing, the seat of transcendent glory, to rain down upon us, and upon Thy servants, the overflowing rain of Thy mercy, that it may cleanse us from the remembrance of all else but Thee, and draw us nigh unto the shores of the ocean of Thy grace. Ordain, O Lord, through Thy most exalted Pen, that which will immortalize our souls in the Realm of glory, will perpetuate our names in Thy Kingdom, and safeguard our lives in the treasuries of Thy protection and our bodies in the stronghold of Thy inviolable fastness. Powerful art Thou over all things, be they of the past or of the future. No God is there but Thee, the omnipotent Protector, the Self-Subsisting.

Thou seest, O Lord, our suppliant hands lifted up towards the heaven of Thy favour and bounty. Grant that they may be filled with the treasures of Thy munificence and bountiful favour. Forgive us, and our fathers, and our mothers, and fulfil whatsoever we have desired from the ocean of Thy grace and Divine generosity. Accept, O Beloved of our hearts, all our works in Thy path. Thou art, verily, the Most Powerful, the Most Exalted, the Incomparable, the One, the Forgiving, the Gracious.

BAHÁ'U'LLÁH

6

PRAISED be Thou, O Lord my God! I supplicate Thee by Him Whom Thou hast called into being, Whose Revelation Thou hast ordained to be Thine own Revelation and His Concealment Thine own Concealment. Through His Firstness Thou hast confirmed Thine own Firstness, and through His Lastness Thou hast affirmed Thine own Lastness. Through the power of His might and the influence of His sovereignty the mighty have apprehended Thine omnipotence, and through His glory they who are endowed with authority have acknowledged Thy majesty and greatness. Through His supreme ascendancy Thy transcendent sovereignty and all-encompassing dominion have been recognized, and through His will Thine own will hath been revealed. Through the light of His countenance the splendours of Thine own face have shone forth, and through His Cause Thine own Cause hath been made manifest. Through the generative power of His utterance the whole earth hath been made the recipient of the wondrous signs and tokens of Thy sovereignty, and the heavens have been filled with the revelations of Thine incomparable majesty, and the seas have been enriched with the sacred pearls of Thine omniscience and wisdom, and the trees adorned with the fruits of Thy knowledge. Through Him all things have sung Thy praise, and all the eyes have been turned in the direction of Thy mercy. Through Him the faces of all have been set towards the splendours of the light of Thy countenance, and the souls of all have been inclined unto the revelations of Thy divine greatness.

How great is Thy power! How exalted Thy sovereignty! How lofty Thy might! How excellent Thy majesty! How supreme is Thy grandeur – a grandeur which He Who is Thy Manifestation hath made known and wherewith Thou hast invested Him as a sign of Thy generosity and bountiful favour. I bear witness, O my God, that through Him Thy most resplendent signs have been uncovered, and Thy mercy hath encompassed the entire creation. But for Him, how could the Celestial Dove have uttered its songs or the Heavenly Nightingale, according to the decree of God, have warbled its melody?

I testify that no sooner had the First Word proceeded, through the potency of Thy will and purpose, out of His mouth, and the First Call gone forth from His lips than the whole creation was revolutionized, and all that are in the heavens and all that are on earth were stirred to the depths. Through that Word the realities of all created things were shaken, were divided, separated, scattered, combined and reunited, disclosing, in both the contingent world and the heavenly kingdom, entities of a new creation, and revealing, in the unseen realms, the signs and tokens of Thy unity and oneness. Through that Call Thou didst announce unto all Thy servants the advent of Thy most great Revelation and the appearance of Thy most perfect Cause.

No sooner had that Revelation been unveiled to men's eyes than the signs of universal discord appeared among the peoples of the world, and commotion seized the dwellers of earth and heaven, and the foundations of all things were shaken. The forces of dissension were released, the meaning of the Word was unfolded, and every several atom in all created things acquired its own distinct and separate character. Hell was made to blaze, and the delights of Paradise were uncovered to men's eyes. Blessed is the man that turneth towards Thee, and woe betide him who standeth aloof from Thee, who denieth Thee and repudiateth Thy signs in this Revelation wherein the faces of the exponents of denial have turned black and the faces of the exponents of truthfulness have turned white, O Thou Who art the Possessor of all names and attributes, Who holdest in Thy grasp the empire of whatever hath been created in heaven and on earth!

Praise be to Thee, therefore, O my God – such praise as Thou didst ascribe to Thine own Self, and which none except Thee can either comprehend or reckon. Thou art He, O my Lord, Who hath made known His own Self unto me, at a time when Thy servants have failed to recognize Thee – servants who, by virtue of the ties that bind them to Thee, have been ruling over all that dwell on earth and have been vaunting themselves over its peoples. Were I, O my God, to exercise from pole to pole supreme dominion over the earth, and were I to be offered all the treasures it containeth, and were I to expend them in Thy path, I would still be powerless to attain unto this station, unless I were assisted and strengthened by Thee. And were I to glorify Thee, O my God, so long as the glory of Thy majesty endureth and the influence of Thy sovereignty and power will last, such a glorification could never be compared with any of the praises which Thou, as a token of Thy grace, hast taught me, and wherewith Thou hast bidden me to extol Thy virtues. If such be the excellence of each one of the praises which Thou hast taught me, how immeasurably greater must be the excellence of the station of the One Who hath known Thee, Who hath entered Thy Presence, and pursued steadfastly the path of Thy Cause!

I have clearly perceived, and I am wholly persuaded, that Thou hast from everlasting been immeasurably exalted above the mention of all beings, and wilt continue unto everlasting to remain far above the conception of Thy creatures. None can befittingly praise Thee except Thine own Self and such as are like unto Thee. Thou hast, verily, been at all times, and wilt everlastingly continue to remain, immensely exalted beyond and above all comparison and likeness, above all imagination of parity or resemblance. Having, thus, recognized Thee as One Who is incomparable, and Whose nature none can possess, it becometh incontrovertibly evident that whosoever may praise Thee, his praise can befit only such as are of his own nature, and are subject to his own limitations, and it can in no wise adequately describe the sublimity of Thy sovereignty, nor scale the heights of Thy majesty and holiness. How sweet, therefore, is the praise Thou givest to Thine own Self, and the description Thou givest of Thine own Being!

I testify, O my God, that Thou hast, from eternity, sent down upon Thy servants naught else except that which can cause them to soar up and be drawn near unto Thee, and to ascend into the heaven of Thy transcendent oneness. Thou hast established Thy bounds among them, and ordained them to stand among Thy creatures as evidences of Thy justice and as signs of Thy mercy, and to be the stronghold of Thy protection amongst Thy people, that no man may in Thy realm transgress against his neighbour. How great is the blessedness of him who, for love of Thy beauty and for the sake of Thy pleasure, hath curbed the desires of a corrupt inclination and observed the precepts laid down by Thy most exalted Pen! He, in truth, is to be numbered with them that have attained unto all good, and followed the way of guidance.

I beseech Thee, O my Lord, by Thy Name through which Thou hast enabled Thy servants and Thy people to know Thee, through which Thou hast drawn the hearts of those who have recognized Thee towards the resplendent court of Thy oneness, and the souls of Thy favoured ones unto the Day-Spring of Thy unity, – I beseech Thee to grant that I may be assisted to observe the fast wholly for Thy sake, O Thou Who art full of majesty and glory! Empower me, then, O my God, to be reckoned among them that have clung to Thy laws and precepts for the sake of Thee alone, their eyes fixed on Thy face. These, indeed, are they whose wine is all that hath proceeded out of the mouth of Thy primal will, whose pure beverage is Thine enthralling call, whose heavenly River is Thy love, whose Paradise is entrance into Thy presence and reunion with Thee. For Thou hast been their Beginning and their End, and their Highest Hope, and their Supreme Desire. Blinded be the eye that gazeth on whatsoever may displease Thee, and confounded be the soul that seeketh the things that are contrary to Thy will.

Deign, O my God, I implore Thee, by Thy Self and by them, to accept, through Thy grace and Thy loving-kindness, the works we have performed, however much they fall short of the loftiness of Thy state and the sublimity of Thy station, O Thou Who art most dear to the hearts that long for Thee, and the Healer of the souls that have recognized Thee! Rain down, therefore, upon us from the heaven of Thy mercy and the clouds of Thy gracious providence that which will cleanse us from the faintest trace of evil and corrupt desires, and will draw us nearer unto Him Who is the Manifestation of Thy most exalted and all-glorious Self. Thou art, verily, the Lord of this world and of the next, and art powerful to do all things.

Do Thou bless, O Lord my God, the Primal Point, through Whom the point of creation hath been made to revolve in both the visible and invisible worlds, Whom Thou hast designated as the One whereunto should return whatsoever must return unto Thee, and as the Revealer of whatsoever may be manifested by Thee. Do Thou also bless such of His Letters as have not turned away from Thee, who have been firmly established in Thy love, and clung steadfastly to Thy good-pleasure. Bless Thou, likewise, as long as Thine own Self endureth and Thine own Essence doth last, them that have suffered martyrdom in Thy path. Thou art, verily, the Ever-Forgiving, the Most Merciful.

Moreover, I beseech Thee, O my God, by Him Whom Thou hast announced unto us in all Thy Tablets and Thy Books and Thy Scrolls and Thy Scriptures, through Whom the kingdom of names hath been convulsed, and all that lay hid in the breasts of them that have followed their evil and corrupt desires hath been revealed, – I beseech Thee to strengthen us in our love for Him, to make us steadfast in His Cause, to help us befriend His loved ones and challenge His enemies. Shield us, then, O my God, from the mischief wrought by them that have denied Thy presence, and turned away from Thy face, and resolved to put an end to the life of Him Who is the Manifestation of Thine own Self.

O my God and my Master! Thou knowest how they have disgraced Thy Cause and dishonoured Thee among Thy creatures, how they have joined Thine enemies, that they may undermine Thy Revelation and injure Thee. Lay hold on them with the power of Thy wrath and might, O my God, and expose their shameful acts and their wickedness, that whatever is hid in their breasts may be revealed unto the people that dwell within Thy land, O Thou Who art the Inflictor of trials, the Fashioner of nations, and the Bestower of favours! No God is there beside Thee, the All-Glorious, the Most Bountiful.

BAHÁ'U'LLÁH

7

O DIVINE Providence! As I am abstaining from bodily desires and not occupied with eating and drinking, even so purify and sanctify my heart from the love of anyone save Thyself and shield and protect my soul from corrupt desires and satanic qualities so that my spirit may commune with the breaths of holiness and fast from the mention of all else besides Thee.

'ABDU'L-BAHÁ

SELECTED PRAYERS
revealed by
BAHÁ'U'LLÁH, THE BÁB AND 'ABDU'L-BAHÁ

O MY God and my Master! I am Thy servant and the son of Thy servant. I have risen from my couch at this dawn-tide when the Day-Star of Thy oneness hath shone forth from the Day-Spring of Thy will, and hath shed its radiance upon the whole world, according to what had been ordained in the Books of Thy Decree.

Praise be unto Thee, O my God, that we have wakened to the splendours of the light of Thy knowledge. Send down, then, upon us, O my Lord, what will enable us to dispense with any one but Thee, and will rid us of all attachment to aught except Thyself. Write down, moreover, for me, and for such as are dear to me, and for my kindred, man and woman alike, the good of this world and the world to come. Keep us safe, then, through Thine unfailing protection, O Thou the Beloved of the entire creation and the Desire of the whole universe, from them whom Thou hast made to be the manifestations of the Evil Whisperer, who whisper in men's breasts. Potent art Thou to do Thy pleasure. Thou art, verily, the Almighty, the Help in Peril, the Self-Subsisting.

Bless Thou, O Lord my God, Him Whom Thou hast set over Thy most excellent Titles, and through Whom Thou hast divided between the godly and the wicked, and graciously aid us to do what Thou lovest and desirest. Bless Thou, moreover, O my God, them Who are Thy Words and Thy Letters, and them who have set their faces towards Thee, and turned unto Thy face, and hearkened to Thy Call.

Thou art, truly, the Lord and King of all men and art potent over all things.

BAHÁ'U'LLÁH

2

LAUDED be Thy name, O my God! I am so carried away by the breezes blowing from Thy presence that I have forgotten my self and all that I possess. This is but a sign of the wonders of Thy grace and bountiful favours vouchsafed unto me. I give praise to Thee, O my God, that Thou hast chosen me out of all Thy creatures, and made me to be the Day-Spring of Thy strength and the Manifestation of Thy might, and empowered me to reveal such of Thy signs and such tokens of Thy majesty and power as none, whether in Thy heaven or on Thy earth, can produce.

I beseech Thee, O my Lord, by Thy most effulgent Name, to acquaint my people with the things Thou didst destine for them. Do Thou, then, preserve them within the stronghold of Thy guardianship and the tabernacle of Thine unerring protection, lest through them may appear what will divide Thy servants. Assemble them, O my Lord, on the shores of this Ocean, every drop of which proclaimeth Thee to be God, besides Whom there is none other God, the All-Glorious, the All-Wise.

Uncover before them, O my Lord, the majesty of Thy Cause, lest they be led to doubt Thy sovereignty and the power of Thy might. I swear by Thy glory, O Thou Who art the Beloved of the worlds! Had they been aware of Thy power they would of a certainty have refused to utter what Thou didst not ordain for them in the heaven of Thy will.

Inspire them, O my Lord, with a sense of their own powerlessness before Him Who is the Manifestation of Thy Self, and teach them to recognize the poverty of their own nature in the face of the manifold tokens of Thy self-sufficiency and riches, that they may gather together round Thy Cause, and cling to the hem of Thy mercy, and cleave to the cord of the good-pleasure of Thy will.

Thou art the Lord of the worlds, and of all those who show mercy, art the Most Merciful.

BAHÁ'U'LLÁH

3

FROM the sweet-scented streams of Thine eternity give me to drink, O my God, and of the fruits of the tree of Thy being enable me to taste, O my Hope! From the crystal springs of Thy love suffer me to quaff, O my Glory, and beneath the shadow of Thine everlasting providence let me abide, O my Light! Within the meadows of Thy nearness, before Thy presence, make me able to roam, O my Beloved, and at the right hand of the throne of Thy mercy seat me, O my Desire! From the fragrant breezes of Thy joy let a breath pass over me, O my Goal, and into the heights of the paradise of Thy reality let me gain admission, O my Adored One! To the melodies of the dove of Thy oneness suffer me to hearken, O Resplendent One, and through the spirit of Thy power and Thy might quicken me, O my Provider! In the spirit of Thy love keep me steadfast, O my Succourer, and in the path of Thy good-pleasure set firm my steps, O my Maker! Within the garden of Thine immortality, before Thy countenance, let me abide for ever, O Thou Who art merciful unto me, and upon the seat of Thy glory stablish me, O Thou Who art my Possessor! To the heaven of Thy loving-kindness lift me up, O my Quickener, and unto the Day-Star of Thy guidance lead me, O Thou my Attractor! Before the revelations of Thine invisible spirit summon me to be present, O Thou Who art my Origin and my Highest Wish, and unto the essence of the fragrance of Thy beauty, which Thou wilt manifest, cause me to return, O Thou Who art my God!

Potent art Thou to do what pleaseth Thee. Thou art, verily, the Most Exalted, the All-Glorious, the All-Highest.

BAHÁ'U'LLÁH

4

O GOD, Who art the Author of all Manifestations, the Source of all Sources, the Fountain-Head of all Revelations, and the Well-Spring of all Lights! I testify that by Thy Name the heaven of understanding hath been adorned, and the ocean of utterance hath surged, and the dispensations of Thy providence have been promulgated unto the followers of all religions.

I beseech Thee so to enrich me as to dispense with all save Thee, and be made independent of any one except Thyself. Rain down, then, upon me out of the clouds of Thy bounty that which shall profit me in every world of Thy worlds. Assist me, then, through Thy strengthen-

ing grace, so to serve Thy Cause amidst Thy servants
that I may show forth what will cause me to be
remembered as long as Thine own kingdom endureth
and Thy dominion will last.

This is Thy servant, O my Lord, who with his whole
being hath turned unto the horizon of Thy bounty, and
the ocean of Thy grace, and the heaven of Thy gifts. Do
with me then as becometh Thy majesty, and Thy glory,
and Thy bounteousness, and Thy grace.

Thou, in truth, art the God of strength and power,
Who art meet to answer them that pray Thee. There is
no God save Thee, the All-Knowing, the All-Wise.

BAHÁ'U'LLÁH

5

LAUDED be Thy name, O my God and the God of all
things, my Glory and the Glory of all things, my Desire
and the Desire of all things, my Strength and the
Strength of all things, my King and the King of all
things, my Possessor and the Possessor of all things, my
Aim and the Aim of all things, my Mover and the
Mover of all things! Suffer me not, I implore Thee, to
be kept back from the ocean of Thy tender mercies, nor
to be far removed from the shores of nearness to Thee.

Aught else except Thee, O my Lord, profiteth me
not, and near access to any one save Thyself availeth me
nothing. I entreat Thee by the plenteousness of Thy
riches, whereby Thou didst dispense with all else except
Thyself, to number me with such as have set their faces
towards Thee, and arisen to serve Thee.

Forgive, then, O my Lord, Thy servants and Thy

handmaidens. Thou, truly, art the Ever-Forgiving, the Most Compassionate.

BAHÁ'U'LLÁH

6

PRAISE be unto Thee, O my God! Thou art He Who by a word of His mouth hath revolutionized the entire creation, and by a stroke of His pen hath divided Thy servants one from another. I bear witness, O my God, that through a word spoken by Thee in this Revelation all created things were made to expire, and through yet another word all such as Thou didst wish were, by Thy grace and bounty, endued with new life.

I render Thee thanks, therefore, and extol Thee, in the name of all them that are dear to Thee, for that Thou hast caused them to be born again, by reason of the living waters which have flowed down out of the mouth of Thy will. Since Thou didst quicken them by Thy bounteousness, O my God, make them steadfastly inclined, through Thy graciousness, towards Thy will; and since Thou didst suffer them to enter into the Tabernacle of Thy Cause, grant by Thy grace that they may not be kept back from Thee.

Unlock, then, to their hearts, O my God, the portals of Thy knowledge, that they may recognize Thee as One Who is far above the reach and ken of the understanding of Thy creatures, and immeasurably exalted above the strivings of Thy people to hint at Thy nature, and may not follow every clamorous impostor that presumeth to speak in Thy name. Enable them, moreover, O my Lord, to cleave so tenaciously to Thy

Cause that they may remain unmoved by the perplexing suggestions of them who, prompted by their desires, utter what hath been forbidden unto them in Thy Tablets and Thy Scriptures.

Thou art well aware, O my Lord, that I hear the howling of the wolves which appear in Thy servants' clothing. Keep safe, therefore, Thy loved ones from their mischief, and enable them to cling steadfastly to whatsoever hath been manifested by Thee in this Revelation, which no other Revelation within Thy knowledge hath excelled.

Do Thou destine for them, O my Lord, that which will profit them. Illumine, then, their eyes with the light of Thy knowledge, that they may see Thee visibly supreme over all things, and resplendent amidst Thy creatures, and victorious over all that are in Thy heaven and all that are on Thy earth. Powerful art Thou to do Thy pleasure. No God is there but Thee, the All-Glorious, Whose help is implored by all men.

Praised be Thou, Who art the Lord of all creation.

BAHÁ'U'LLÁH

7

GLORIFIED art Thou, O my God! I yield Thee thanks that Thou hast made known unto me Him Who is the Day-Spring of Thy mercy, and the Dawning-Place of Thy grace, and the Repository of Thy Cause. I beseech Thee by Thy Name, through which the faces of them that are nigh unto Thee have turned white, and the hearts of such as are devoted to Thee have winged their flight towards Thee, to grant that I may, at all times and under all conditions, lay hold on Thy cord, and be rid of all attachment to any one except Thee, and may keep mine eyes directed towards the horizon of Thy Revelation, and may carry out what Thou hast prescribed unto me in Thy Tablets.

Attire, O my Lord, both my inner and outer being with the raiment of Thy favours and Thy loving-kindness. Keep me safe, then, from whatsoever may be abhorrent unto Thee, and graciously assist me and my kindred to obey Thee, and to shun whatsoever may stir up any evil or corrupt desire within me.

Thou, truly, art the Lord of all mankind, and the Possessor of this world and of the next. No God is there save Thee, the All-Knowing, the All-Wise.

BAHÁ'U'LLÁH

8

O THOU Whose nearness is my wish, Whose presence is my hope, Whose remembrance is my desire, Whose court of glory is my goal, Whose abode is my aim, Whose name is my healing, Whose love is the radiance of my heart, Whose service is my highest aspiration! I beseech Thee by Thy Name, through which Thou hast enabled them that have recognized Thee to soar to the sublimest heights of the knowledge of Thee and empowered such as devoutly worship Thee to ascend into the precincts of the court of Thy holy favours, to aid me to turn my face towards Thy face, to fix mine eyes upon Thee, and to speak of Thy glory.

I am the one, O my Lord, who hath forgotten all else but Thee, and turned towards the Day-Spring of Thy grace, who hath forsaken all save Thyself in the hope of drawing nigh unto Thy court. Behold me, then, with mine eyes lifted up towards the Seat that shineth with the splendours of the light of Thy Face. Send down, then, upon me, O my Beloved, that which will enable me to be steadfast in Thy Cause, so that the doubts of the infidels may not hinder me from turning towards Thee.

Thou art, verily, the God of Power, the Help in Peril, the All-Glorious, the Almighty.

BAHÁ'U'LLÁH

9

LAUDED be Thy name, O Lord my God! Thou seest how I have turned myself toward Thee, and set my face in the direction of Thy grace and Thy gifts. I implore Thee, by Thy name through which Thou didst enable all them that have recognized Thy unity to partake of the wine of Thy mercy, and all such as have drawn nigh unto Thee to quaff the living waters of Thy loving-kindness, to rid me entirely of all vain imaginings, and to incline me in the direction of Thy grace, O Thou Who art the Lord of all men!

Graciously assist me, O my God, in the days of the Manifestation of Thy Cause and of the Day-Spring of Thy Revelation, to tear asunder the veils which have hindered me from recognizing Thee, and from immersing myself beneath the ocean of Thy knowledge. Hold Thou me with the hands of Thy power, and grant that I may be so carried away by the sweet melodies of the

Dove of Thy oneness, that I will cease to regard in all creation any face except Thy face, O Thou the Goal of my desire, and will recognize in the visible world naught else save the evidences of Thy might, O Thou Who art the God of mercy!

I am but a wretched creature, O my Lord, and Thou art the All-Possessing, the Most High; and I am all weakness, and Thou art the Almighty, and the Supreme Ordainer in both the beginning and the end. Withhold not from me the fragrances of Thy Revelation, and shatter not my hopes in the outpourings which have been sent down out of the heaven of Thy gifts. Ordain Thou for me, O my God, the good of this world and the world to come, and grant me what will profit me in every world of Thy worlds, for I know not what will help or harm me. Thou, in truth, art the All-Knowing, the All-Wise.

Have mercy, then, O my God, upon Thy servants who are drowned in the midst of the ocean of evil suggestions, and deliver them by the power of Thy sovereignty, O Thou Who art the Lord of all names and attributes! Thou art He Who from everlasting hath ordained what hath pleased Thee, and will unto everlasting abide the same. No God is there but Thee, the Ever-Forgiving, the Most Merciful.

BAHÁ'U'LLÁH

10

LAUDED and glorified art Thou, O my God! I entreat Thee by the sighing of Thy lovers and by the tears shed by them that long to behold Thee, not to withhold from me Thy tender mercies in Thy Day, nor to deprive me of the melodies of the Dove that extolleth Thy oneness before the light that shineth from Thy face. I am the one who is in misery, O God! Behold me cleaving fast to Thy Name, the All-Possessing. I am the one who is sure to perish; behold me clinging to Thy Name, the Imperishable. I implore Thee, therefore, by Thy Self, the Exalted, the Most High, not to abandon me unto mine own self and unto the desires of a corrupt inclination. Hold Thou my hand with the hand of Thy power, and deliver me from the depths of my fancies and idle imaginings, and cleanse me of all that is abhorrent unto Thee.

Cause me, then, to turn wholly unto Thee, to put my whole trust in Thee, to seek Thee as my Refuge, and to flee unto Thy face. Thou art, verily, He Who, through the power of His might, doeth whatsoever He desireth, and commandeth, through the potency of His will, whatsoever He chooseth. None can withstand the operation of Thy decree; none can divert the course of Thine appointment. Thou art, in truth, the Almighty, the All-Glorious, the Most Bountiful.

BAHÁ'U'LLÁH

I I

PRAISED and glorified art Thou, O God! Grant that the day of attaining Thy holy presence may be fast approaching. Cheer our hearts through the potency of Thy love and good-pleasure, and bestow upon us steadfastness that we may willingly submit to Thy Will and Thy Decree. Verily, Thy knowledge embraceth all the things Thou hast created or wilt create, and Thy celestial might transcendeth whatsoever Thou hast called or wilt call into being. There is none to be worshipped but Thee, there is none to be desired except Thee, there is none to be adored besides Thee and there is naught to be loved save Thy good-pleasure.

Verily, Thou art the supreme Ruler, the Sovereign Truth, the Help in Peril, the Self-Subsisting.

THE BÁB

12

THE glory of glories and the most resplendent light rest upon Thee, O my God. Thy majesty is so transcendent that no human imagination can reach it and Thy consummate power is so sublime that the birds of men's hearts and minds can never attain its heights. All beings acknowledge their powerlessness to praise Thee as beseemeth Thy station. Immeasurably exalted art Thou. No one can glorify Thy Being, or fathom the evidences of Thy bounty as it exists in Thine inmost Essence, since Thou alone knowest Thyself as Thou art in Thyself.

I yield praise unto Thee, O Lord our God, for the bounty of having called into being the realm of creation and invention – a praise which shineth resplendent through the potency of Thine inspiration which none other but Thee can befittingly appraise. I glorify Thee moreover and render Thee thanks as beseemeth Thine awe-inspiring presence and the glory of Thine over-powering majesty, for this sublime blessing, this

wondrous sign which is manifest in Thy kingdoms of
Revelation and Creation.

All glory be unto Thee. Immeasurably exalted is that
which beseemeth Thee. Verily no one hath ever
adequately grasped the loftiness of Thy station, nor hath
any one except Thee recognized Thee as beseemeth
Thee. Thou art manifest through the outpourings of
Thy bounty, while no one besides Thee can fathom the
sublimity of Thy Revelation.

Magnified be Thy name. Hath aught else save Thee
any independent existence so as to be capable of hinting
at Thy nature, and doth anyone but Thee possess any
trace of identity wherewith I could recognize Thee? All
that is known owes its renown to the splendour of Thy
Name, the Most Manifest, and every object is deeply
stirred by the vibrating influence emanating from Thine
invincible Will. Thou art nearer unto all things than all
things.

Lauded and glorified art Thou. Too exalted is Thy
loftiness for the hands of such as are endued with
understanding to reach unto Thee, and too profound is
Thy fathomless depth for the rivers of men's minds and
perceptions to flow out therefrom.

THE BÁB

13

O MY God! There is no one but Thee to allay the
anguish of my soul, and Thou art my highest aspiration,
O my God. My heart is wedded to none save Thee and
such as Thou dost love. I solemnly declare that my life

and death are both for Thee. Verily Thou art incomparable and hast no partner.

O my Lord! I beg Thee to forgive me for shutting myself out from Thee. By Thy glory and majesty, I have failed to befittingly recognize Thee and to worship Thee, while Thou dost make Thyself known unto me and callest me to remembrance as beseemeth Thy station. Grievous woe would betide me, O my Lord, wert Thou to take hold of me by reason of my misdeeds and trespasses. No helper do I know of other than Thee. No refuge do I have to flee to save Thee. None among Thy creatures can dare to intercede with Thyself without Thy leave. I hold fast to Thy love before Thy court, and, according to Thy bidding, I earnestly pray unto Thee as befitteth Thy glory. I beg Thee to heed my call as Thou hast promised me. Verily Thou art God; no God is there but Thee. Alone and unaided, Thou art independent of all created things. Neither can the devotion of Thy lovers profit Thee, nor the evil doings of the faithless harm Thee. Verily Thou art my God, He Who will never fail in His promise.

O my God! I beseech Thee by the evidences of Thy favour, to let me draw nigh to the sublime heights of Thy holy presence, and protect me from inclining myself toward the subtle allusions of aught else but Thee. Guide my steps, O my God, unto that which is acceptable and pleasing to Thee. Shield me, through Thy might, from the fury of Thy wrath and chastisement, and hold me back from entering habitations not desired by Thee.

THE BÁB

14

IMMEASURABLY exalted art Thou, O my God, above the endeavours of all beings and created things to praise Thee and recognize Thee. No creature can ever comprehend Thee as beseemeth the reality of Thy holy Being and no servant can ever worship Thee as is worthy of Thine unknowable Essence. Praise be unto Thee; too high is Thine exalted Self for any allusions proceeding from Thy creatures ever to gain access unto Thy presence.

Whenever, O my God, I soared into Thy holy atmosphere and attained the inmost spirit of prayerfulness unto Thee, I was led to recognize that Thou art inaccessible and that no mention of Thee can ever reach Thy transcendent court. Therefore I turn towards Thy Loved Ones – They upon Whom Thou hast graciously conferred Thine Own station that They might manifest Thy love and Thy true knowledge. Bless Them then, O my God, with every distinction and goodly gift which Thy knowledge may reckon within the domain of Thy power.

O my God, my Lord and my Master! I swear by Thy might and glory that Thou alone and no one else besides Thee art the ultimate Desire of all men, and that Thou alone and none other save Thee art the Object of adoration. O my God! The paths of Thine inaccessible glory have prompted me to voice these words and the ways of Thine unattainable heights have guided me to make these allusions. Exalted art Thou, O my God! The evidences of Thy revelation are too manifest for me to need to refer to aught else save Thyself, and the love I cherish for Thee is far sweeter to my taste than the knowledge of all things and freeth me from the need to seek anyone's knowledge other than Thine.

All praise be unto Thee, O my Lord. I verily believe in Thee, as Thou art in Thyself; and of Thee, as Thou art in Thyself, I beg forgiveness for myself and on behalf of all mankind.

O my God! Wholly have I fled unto Thy face and have cast myself before Thee and no power have I over aught in Thy holy presence. Shouldst Thou chastise me with Thy might, Thou wouldst assuredly be just in Thy decree; and wert Thou to bestow every goodly gift on me, Thou wouldst indeed be most generous and bountiful. Verily Thou art independent of all the peoples of the world.

I have sought reunion with Thee, O my Master, yet have I failed to attain thereto save through the knowledge of detachment from aught save Thee. I have yearned for Thy love, but failed to find it except in renouncing everything other than Thyself. I have been eager to worship Thee, yet have I failed to achieve Thy adoration, except by loving those who cherish Thy love. No one do I recognize, O my God, except Thee. Thou art incomparable and hast no partner. Thou alone knowest our shortcomings and none other hath this knowledge. I beg Thy forgiveness for whatever doth displease Thee.

I call upon Thee at all times with the tongue of Thine inspiration, saying: 'Thou art in truth the All-Possessing, the Peerless. No God is there but Thee. Immeasurably far and exalted art Thou above the descriptions of those who arrogantly assign peers unto Thee.'

THE BÁB

15

O Lord! Unto Thee I repair for refuge, and toward all Thy signs I set my heart.

O Lord! Whether travelling or at home, and in my occupation or in my work, I place my whole trust in Thee.

Grant me then Thy sufficing help so as to make me independent of all things, O Thou Who art unsurpassed in Thy mercy!

Bestow upon me my portion, O Lord, as Thou pleasest, and cause me to be satisfied with whatsoever Thou hast ordained for me.

Thine is the absolute authority to command.

THE BÁB

16

THROUGHOUT eternity Thou hast been, O my Lord, and wilt ever remain the One true God, while all else save Thee are needy and poor. Having clung tenaciously to Thy Cord, O my God, I have detached myself from all mankind, and having set my face towards the habitation of Thy tender mercy, I have turned away from all created things. Graciously inspire me, O my God, through Thy grace and bounty, Thy glory and majesty, and Thy dominion and grandeur, for no one mighty and all-knowing can I find beside Thee. Protect me, O my God, through the potency of Thy transcendent and all-sufficing glory and by the hosts of the heavens and the earth, inasmuch as in no one can I wholly place my trust but in Thee and no refuge is there but Thee.

Thou art God, my Lord, Thou knowest my needs, Thou seest my state and art well aware of what hath befallen me by reason of Thy decree, and of the earthly sufferings I have endured by Thy leave and as a token of Thy bounty and favour.

THE BÁB

17

I BEG Thee to forgive me, O my Lord, for every mention but the mention of Thee, and for every praise but the praise of Thee, and for every delight but delight in Thy nearness, and for every pleasure but the pleasure of communion with Thee, and for every joy but the joy of Thy love and of Thy good-pleasure, and for all things pertaining unto me which bear no relationship unto Thee, O Thou Who art the Lord of lords, He Who provideth the means and unlocketh the doors.

THE BÁB

18

VOUCHSAFE unto me, O my God, the full measure of Thy love and Thy good-pleasure, and through the attractions of Thy resplendent light enrapture our hearts, O Thou Who art the Supreme Evidence and the All-Glorified. Send down upon me, as a token of Thy grace, Thy vitalizing breezes, throughout the day-time and in the night season, O Lord of bounty.

No deed have I done, O my God, to merit beholding

Thy face, and I know of a certainty that were I to live as long as the world lasts I would fail to accomplish any deed such as to deserve this favour, inasmuch as the station of a servant shall ever fall short of access to Thy holy precincts, unless Thy bounty should reach me and Thy tender mercy pervade me and Thy loving-kindness encompass me.

All praise be unto Thee, O Thou besides Whom there is none other God. Graciously enable me to ascend unto Thee, to be granted the honour of dwelling in Thy nearness and to have communion with Thee alone. No God is there but Thee.

Indeed shouldst Thou desire to confer blessing upon a servant Thou wouldst blot out from the realm of his heart every mention or disposition except Thine Own mention; and shouldst Thou ordain evil for a servant by reason of that which his hands have unjustly wrought before Thy face, Thou wouldst test him with the benefits of this world and of the next that he might become preoccupied therewith and forget Thy remembrance.

THE BÁB

19

ALL majesty and glory, O my God, and all dominion and light and grandeur and splendour be unto Thee. Thou bestowest sovereignty on whom Thou willest and dost withhold it from whom Thou desirest. No God is there but Thee, the All-Possessing, the Most Exalted. Thou art He Who createth from naught the universe and all that dwell therein. There is nothing worthy of Thee except Thyself, while all else but Thee are as outcasts in Thy holy presence and are as nothing when compared to the glory of Thine Own Being.

Far be it from me to extol Thy virtues save by what Thou hast extolled Thyself in Thy weighty Book where Thou sayest, 'No vision taketh in Him but He taketh in all vision. He is the Subtile, the All-Perceiving.'* Glory be unto Thee, O my God, indeed no mind or vision, however keen or discriminating, can ever grasp the nature of the most insignificant of Thy signs. Verily Thou art God, no God is there besides Thee. I bear witness that Thou Thyself alone art the sole expression of Thine attributes, that the praise of no one besides Thee can ever attain to Thy holy court nor can Thine attributes ever be fathomed by anyone other than Thyself.

Glory be unto Thee, Thou art exalted above the description of anyone save Thyself, since it is beyond human conception to befittingly magnify Thy virtues or to comprehend the inmost reality of Thine Essence. Far be it from Thy glory that Thy creatures should describe Thee or that any one besides Thyself should ever know Thee. I have known Thee, O my God, by reason of Thy making Thyself known unto me, for hadst Thou not revealed Thyself unto me, I would not have known Thee. I worship Thee by virtue of Thy summoning me unto Thee, for had it not been for Thy summons I would not have worshipped Thee. Lauded art Thou, O my God, my trespasses have waxed mighty and my sins have assumed grievous proportions. How disgraceful my plight will prove to be in Thy holy presence. I have failed to know Thee to the extent Thou didst reveal Thyself unto me; I have failed to worship Thee with a devotion worthy of Thy summons; I have failed to obey

* Qur'án 6:103

Thee through not treading the path of Thy love in the manner Thou didst inspire me.

Thy might beareth me witness, O my God, what befitteth Thee is far greater and more exalted than any being could attempt to accomplish. Indeed nothing can ever comprehend Thee as is worthy of Thee nor can any servile creature worship Thee as beseemeth Thine adoration. So perfect and comprehensive is Thy proof, O my God, that its inner essence transcendeth the description of any soul and so abundant are the outpourings of Thy gifts that no faculty can appraise their infinite range.

O my God! O my Master! I beseech Thee by Thy manifold bounties and by the pillars which sustain Thy throne of glory, to have pity on these lowly people who are powerless to bear the unpleasant things of this fleeting life, how much less then can they bear Thy chastisement in the life to come – a chastisement which is ordained by Thy justice, called forth by Thy wrath and will continue to exist for ever.

I beg Thee by Thyself, O my God, my Lord and my Master, to intercede in my behalf. I have fled from Thy justice unto Thy mercy. For my refuge I am seeking Thee and such as turn not away from Thy path, even for a twinkling of an eye – they for whose sake Thou didst create the creation as a token of Thy grace and bounty.

THE BÁB

·

20

GLORY be unto Thee, O Lord, Thou Who hast brought into being all created things, through the power of Thy behest.

O Lord! Assist those who have renounced all else but
Thee, and grant them a mighty victory. Send down
upon them, O Lord, the concourse of the angels in
heaven and earth and all that is between, to aid Thy
servants, to succour and strengthen them, to enable
them to achieve success, to sustain them, to invest them
with glory, to confer upon them honour and exaltation,
to enrich them and to make them triumphant with a
wondrous triumph.

Thou art their Lord, the Lord of the heavens and the
earth, the Lord of all the worlds. Strengthen this Faith,
O Lord, through the power of these servants and cause
them to prevail over all the peoples of the world; for
they, of a truth, are Thy servants who have detached
themselves from aught else but Thee, and Thou verily
art the protector of true believers.

Grant Thou, O Lord, that their hearts may, through
allegiance to this, Thine inviolable Faith, grow stronger
than anything else in the heavens and on earth and in
whatsoever is between them; and strengthen, O Lord,
their hands with the tokens of Thy wondrous power
that they may manifest Thy power before the gaze of all
mankind.

THE BÁB

21

O MY God! O my God! Glory be unto Thee for that
Thou hast confirmed me to the confession of Thy
oneness, attracted me unto the word of Thy singleness,
enkindled me by the fire of Thy love, and occupied me
with Thy mention and the service of Thy friends and
maidservants.

O Lord, help me to be meek and lowly, and strengthen me in severing myself from all things and in holding to the hem of the garment of Thy glory, so that my heart may be filled with Thy love and leave no space for love of the world and attachment to its qualities.

O God! Sanctify me from all else save Thee, purge me from the dross of sins and transgressions, and cause me to possess a spiritual heart and conscience.

Verily, Thou art merciful and, verily, Thou art the Most Generous, Whose help is sought by all men.

'ABDU'L-BAHÁ

22

O MY Lord! O my Lord! This is a lamp lighted by the fire of Thy love and ablaze with the flame which is ignited in the tree of Thy mercy. O my Lord! Increase his enkindlement, heat and flame, with the fire which is kindled in the Sinai of Thy Manifestation. Verily, Thou art the Confirmer, the Assister, the Powerful, the Generous, the Loving.

'ABDU'L-BAHÁ

23

O GOD, my God! Thou art my Hope and my Beloved, my highest Aim and Desire! With great humbleness and entire devotion I pray to Thee to make me a minaret of Thy love in Thy land, a lamp of Thy knowledge among

Thy creatures, and a banner of divine bounty in Thy dominion.

Number me with such of Thy servants as have detached themselves from everything but Thee, have sanctified themselves from the transitory things of this world, and have freed themselves from the promptings of the voicers of idle fancies.

Let my heart be dilated with joy through the spirit of confirmation from Thy kingdom, and brighten my eyes by beholding the hosts of divine assistance descending successively upon me from the kingdom of Thine omnipotent glory.

Thou art, in truth, the Almighty, the All-Glorious, the All-Powerful.

'ABDU'L-BAHÁ

24

O GOD! Refresh and gladden my spirit. Purify my heart. Illumine my powers. I lay all my affairs in Thy hand. Thou art my Guide and my Refuge. I will no longer be sorrowful and grieved; I will be a happy and joyful being. O God! I will no longer be full of anxiety, nor will I let trouble harass me. I will not dwell on the unpleasant things of life.

O God! Thou art more friend to me than I am to myself. I dedicate myself to Thee, O Lord.

'ABDU'L-BAHÁ

25

HE is God!

O God, my God! These are servants attracted in Thy days by the fragrances of Thy holiness, enkindled with the flame burning in Thy holy tree, responding to Thy voice, uttering Thy praise, awakened by Thy breeze, stirred by Thy sweet savours, beholding Thy signs, understanding Thy verses, hearkening to Thy words, believing Thy Revelation and assured of Thy loving-kindness. Their eyes, O Lord, are fixed upon Thy kingdom of effulgent glory and their faces turned toward Thy dominion on high, their hearts beating with the love of Thy radiant and glorious beauty, their souls consumed with the flame of Thy love, O Lord of this world and the world hereafter, their lives seething with the ardour of their longing for Thee, and their tears poured forth for Thy sake.

Shield them within the stronghold of Thy protection and safety, preserve them in Thy watchful care, look upon them with the eyes of Thy providence and mercy, make them the signs of Thy divine unity that are manifest throughout all regions, the standards of Thy might that wave above Thy mansions of grandeur, the shining lamps that burn with the oil of Thy wisdom in the globes of Thy guidance, the birds of the garden of Thy knowledge that warble upon the topmost boughs in Thy sheltering paradise, and the leviathans of the ocean of Thy bounty that plunge by Thy supreme mercy in the fathomless deeps.

O Lord, my God! Lowly are these servants of Thine, exalt them in Thy kingdom on high; feeble, strengthen them by Thy supreme power; abased, bestow upon them Thy glory in Thine all-highest realm; poor, enrich them in Thy great dominion. Do Thou then ordain for them all the good Thou hast destined in Thy worlds, visible and invisible, prosper them in this world below, gladden their hearts with Thine inspiration, O Lord of all beings! Illumine their hearts with Thy joyful tidings diffused from Thine all-glorious Station, make firm their steps in Thy Most Great Covenant and strengthen their loins in Thy firm Testament, by Thy bounty and promised grace, O Gracious and Merciful One! Thou art, verily, the Gracious, the All-Bountiful.

'ABDU'L-BAHÁ

PRAYER FOR NAW-RÚZ

PRAISED be Thou, O my God, that Thou hast ordained Naw-Rúz as a festival unto those who have observed the fast for love of Thee and abstained from all that is abhorrent unto Thee. Grant, O my Lord, that the fire of Thy love and the heat produced by the fast enjoined by Thee may inflame them in Thy Cause, and make them to be occupied with Thy praise and with remembrance of Thee.

Since Thou hast adorned them, O my Lord, with the ornament of the fast prescribed by Thee, do Thou adorn them also with the ornament of Thine acceptance, through Thy grace and bountiful favour. For the doings of men are all dependent upon Thy good pleasure, and are conditioned by Thy behest. Shouldst Thou regard him who hath broken the fast as one who hath observed it, such a man would be reckoned among them who from eternity had been keeping the fast. And shouldst Thou decree that he who hath observed the fast hath broken it, that person would be numbered with such as have caused the Robe of Thy Revelation to be stained with dust, and been far removed from the crystal waters of this living Fountain.

Thou art He through Whom the ensign 'Praise-worthy art Thou in Thy works' hath been lifted up, and the standard 'Obeyed art Thou in Thy behest' hath been unfurled. Make known this Thy station, O my God, unto Thy servants, that they may be made aware that the excellence of all things is dependent upon Thy bidding and Thy word, and the virtue of every act is conditioned by Thy leave and the good pleasure of Thy will, and may recognize that the reins of men's doings are within the grasp of Thine acceptance and Thy commandment. Make this known unto them, that nothing whatsoever may shut them out from Thy Beauty, in these days whereon the Christ exclaimeth: 'All dominion is Thine, O Thou the Begetter of the Spirit (Jesus)': and Thy Friend (Muḥammad) crieth out: 'Glory be to Thee, O Thou the Best-Beloved, for that Thou has uncovered Thy Beauty, and written down for Thy chosen ones what will cause them to attain unto the seat of the revelation of Thy Most Great Name, through which all the peoples have lamented except such as have detached themselves from all else except Thee, and set themselves towards Him Who is the Revealer of Thyself and the Manifestation of Thine attributes.'

He Who is Thy Branch and all Thy company, O my Lord, have broken this day their fast, after having observed it within the precincts of Thy court, and in their eagerness to please Thee. Do Thou ordain for Him, and for them, and for all such as have entered Thy presence in those days all the good Thou didst destine in Thy Book. Supply them, then, with that which will profit them, in both this life and in the life beyond.

Thou, in truth, art the All-Knowing, the All-Wise.

BAHÁ'U'LLÁH

REFERENCES

FROM THE WRITINGS OF BAHÁ'U'LLÁH

1   *A Synopsis and Codification of the Kitáb-i-Aqdas* (Haifa: Bahá'í World Centre, 1973), p. 12.
2   ibid. p. 13.
3   ibid.
4   *Tablets of Bahá'u'lláh revealed after the Kitáb-i-Aqdas* (Haifa: Bahá'í World Centre, 1978), pp. 108–9.
5   *Kitáb-i-Íqán* (Wilmette: Bahá'í Publishing Trust, 1960), pp. 38–9.
6   *Gleanings from the Writings of Bahá'u'lláh* (Wilmette: Bahá'í Publishing Trust, 1952), pp. 337–8.

FROM THE WRITINGS OF 'ABDU'L-BAHÁ

1   *Selections from the Writings of 'Abdu'l-Bahá* (Haifa: Bahá'í World Centre, 1978), pp. 69–70.
2   *Bahá'í World Faith* (Wilmette: Bahá'í Publishing Trust, 1956), p. 368 (TAB p. 683).
3   *Tablets of 'Abdu'l-Bahá*, vol. I (Chicago: Bahá'í Publishing Committee, 1909), p. 57.

FROM TABLE TALKS BY 'ABDU'L-BAHÁ

1   From Corinne True, *Table Talks by 'Abdu'l-Bahá* (Chicago, 1907). Published in *Star of the West*, vol. IV, no. 18, p. 305. The closing prayer has been retranslated at the Bahá'í World Centre; the quotation from the *Tablet of Visitation* is in Shoghi Effendi's translation; and transliteration of Persian words has been updated to conform to the system in use at present in the Bahá'í community.
2   Quoted by J.E. Esslemont, *Bahá'u'llah and the New Era* (London, 1923), from Miss E.S. Stevens in *Fortnightly*

Review, June 1911. See p. 189 of the 1970 US edition, and below, 'Reflections on the Fast', No. 7.

FROM LETTERS WRITTEN ON BEHALF OF SHOGHI EFFENDI

1   21 March 1930, in *The World Order of Bahá'u'lláh* (Wilmette: Bahá'í Publishing Trust, 1955), p. 22.

2   17 October 1934, in *Letters from the Guardian to Australia and New Zealand* (Sydney: National Spiritual Assembly of the Bahá'ís of Australia, 1971), p. 6.

3   11 August 1935, to the National Spiritual Assembly of the United States and Canada, in *Bahá'í News*, October 1935, p. 2.

4   10 January 1936, in *Bahá'í News*, March 1936, p. 1.

5   9 March 1937 to an individual believer, cited in a memorandum from the Research Department of the Bahá'í World Centre, 24 August 1987, p. 1.

6   27 October 1938 to an individual believer, in *Bahá'í News*, March 1940, p. 2.

7   May 1943 to an individual believer, in *Unfolding Destiny: The Messages from the Guardian of the Bahá'í Faith to the Bahá'í Community of the British Isles* (London: Bahá'í Publishing Trust, 1981), p. 440.

8   To an individual believer, in *Bahá'í News*, January 1944, p. 2.

9   21 May 1946, in *Unfolding Destiny*, p. 444.

10   To an individual believer, in *Bahá'í News*, October 1948, p. 1.

11   16 March 1949 to an individual believer, quoted in *Living the Life* (London: Bahá'í Publishing Trust, 1974), p. 29.

12   18 February 1950 to an individual believer, in *Unfolding Destiny*, p. 457.

13   18 April 1950 to an individual believer, cited in a memorandum from the Research Department of the Bahá'í World Centre, 24 August 1987, p. 1.

14   To an individual believer, quoted in a letter written on behalf of the Universal House of Justice, 6 November 1985.

FROM *A SYNOPSIS AND CODIFICATION OF THE KITÁB-I-AQDAS*

This section is quoted from *A Synopsis and Codification*, Section IV.B, pp. 38–9, together with its relevant notes. Two additional notes to the passage from letters written on behalf of the Universal House of Justice have also been included.

FROM LETTERS WRITTEN ON BEHALF OF THE UNIVERSAL HOUSE OF JUSTICE

1   From a letter dated 2 March 1986 to an individual believer.

2   From an enclosure to a letter dated 6 November 1985 to an individual believer.

3   From an enclosure to a letter dated 8 July 1981 to an individual believer.

4   From a letter dated 5 January 1972 to the National Spiritual Assembly of the Bahá'ís of New Zealand, quoted in *The Fast* (Auckland: National Spiritual Assembly of the Bahá'ís of New Zealand, 1983), p. 10.

5   From a letter dated 8 August 1969 to the National Spiritual Assembly of the Bahá'ís of the British Isles, quoted in *Lights of Guidance, a Bahá'í Reference File*, ed. Helen Hornby (New Delhi: Bahá'í Publishing Trust, 1983), p. 183.

REFLECTIONS ON THE FAST

1   'An Open Letter to New Bahá'ís Regarding the Fast', *The American Bahá'í*, February 1986, p. 2.

2   *The Desire of the World* (Oxford: George Ronald, 1982), pp. 136–8.

3   *Bahá'í News*, April 1950, p. 2. Written in the year commemorating the hundredth anniversary of the Martyrdom of the Báb.

4   *The Revelation of Bahá'u'lláh: 'Akká, The Early Years* (Oxford: George Ronald, 1983), pp. 293–4.

5   *Miracles and Metaphors* (Los Angeles: Kalimát Press, 1981), pp. 34–5. Translated by Juan Ricardo Cole.

6   Excerpts from *Explanations Concerning Sacred Mysteries*

(Chicago, 1902), published in *Star of the West*, vol. 4, no. 18, pp. 303, 306.

7   *Bahá'u'lláh and the New Era* (London, 1923; Bahá'í Publishing Trust, 1974; Wilmette: Bahá'í Publishing Trust, 1970), pp. 170–71 (UK), 188–9 (US).

8   From 'The Attitude of Bahá'ís Toward Non-Bahá'í Relatives', *Bahá'í News*, January, 1950, p. 9.

9   'Observing the Fast – when you are not to abstain from food', contributed by the compiler for this handbook.

PRAYERS FOR THE FAST

1   Bahá'u'lláh, *Prayers and Meditations* (Wilmette: Bahá'í Publishing Trust, 1938; London: Bahá'í Publishing Trust, 19), no. CLXXVII.

2   ibid. no. LXXXV.

3   ibid. no. VII.

4   ibid. no. LVI.

5   *Gleanings from the Writings of Bahá'u'lláh*, no. CXXXVIII, pp. 299–302.

6   *Prayers and Meditations*, no. CLXXVIII.

7   This passage forms part of the table talk given by 'Abdu'l-Bahá quoted on pp. 15–17 of this book. It has been retranslated at the Bahá'í World Centre.

SELECTED PRAYERS

1   *Prayers and Meditations*, no. CXLIV.

2   ibid. no. XXXVI.

3   ibid. no. CLXV.

4   ibid. no. XLIII.

5   ibid. no. XLII.

6   ibid. no. XXXIII.

7   ibid. no. CXXXVII.

8   ibid. no. CIV.

9   ibid. no. CLXIII.

10   ibid. no. CLXII.

11   *Bahá'í Prayers: A Selection of Prayers Revealed by Bahá'u'lláh, the Báb and 'Abdu'l-Bahá* (Wilmette: Bahá'í Publishing Trust, 1982), p. 166.

12   *Selections from the Writings of the Báb* (Haifa: Bahá'í World Centre, 1976), pp. 194–5.

13   ibid. pp. 204–5.
14   ibid. pp. 200–202.
15   *Bahá'í Prayers*, pp. 56–7.
16   *Selections from the Writings of the Báb*, p. 194.
17   ibid. pp. 182–3.
18   ibid. pp. 191–2.
19   ibid. pp. 202–4.
20   ibid. pp. 192–3.
21   *Bahá'í Prayers*, pp. 152–3.
22   ibid. p. 153
23   ibid. pp. 57–8.
24   ibid. p. 152.
25   ibid. pp. 156–8.

PRAYER FOR NAW-RÚZ

Bahá'í Prayers, pp. 62–4.